CHEST DEEP
And Rising

The Hurricane Katrina Nightmare

Tough times don't last, tough people do!

Patrick

Patrick Yoes

IP

ITHACA PRESS

Ithaca Press
3 Kimberly Drive, Suite B
Dryden, New York 13053 USA
www.IthacaPress.com

Cover Design   Gary Hoffman
Book Design   Gary Hoffman

Cover Photograph by Johnny Frederic
Back Cover Photographs by Thyme Yoes, Joe Labarriere, and
Patrick Yoes
Illustrations by Jairo Leon

Manufactured in the United States of America

9 8 7 6 5 4 3

Library of Congress Control Data Available

Yoes, Patrick
Historical account/Autobiography

First Edition

ISBN: 978-0-9771482-8-8

www.PatrickYoes.com

Dedicated to First Responders in the Gulf South.

They stayed; they reacted; they rescued;

they truly made the difference.

Table of Contents

PART ONE

PART TWO

PART THREE

Acknowledgement

One evening, several months after Hurricane Katrina forever changed the lives of those living in the Gulf South, I received an email with an attachment from a colleague, Charles Guey. He wrote of his experiences as a first responder in Plaquemines Parish during Hurricane Katrina. I was amazed at the detail he provided of the countless rescues and daunting challenges he and the members of the Plaquemines Parish Sheriff's Office had endured. I was even more surprised when he mentioned that he had written the story from memory.

For me, the 16 days of Hurricane Katrina had become a blur, as one day ran into the next. As a first responder in St. Charles Parish, I had lost all sense of time and, with it, the ability to recall the order of events ... or so I had convinced myself. With the initial intent of documenting my involvement and thoughts during this part of American history and sharing it with my children and grandchildren, I decided to give it a try. Fifty pages later, I still hadn't gotten to Katrina's arrival.

Never before had I written anything that caused me to relive events in my life with such detail and emotion. For three months, it became my therapy, a deep reflection into the events that have forever changed me. Still, as family and friends read this story and encouraged the publishing of it, I was reluctant to do so, acknowledging that there were many Hurricane Katrina responders who, because of their selfless actions, were far better deserving to tell this story.

It was the encouragement of my wife, Gail, my daughter, Thyme, and stepdaughter, Denise Pritchard, that persuaded and pushed me to publish this book as an inspiration to others who shared these same experiences. Perhaps they too might be encouraged to share their involvement in this life-changing event.

Although much of this book is about my experiences, many of my colleagues provided their insights and the experiences that are shared in this story. I thank Charles Guey, Tommy Tizzard, Chuck Canterbury, George Breedy, Dwayne Lagrange, Johnny Frederic, Jonathan Walsdorf, Wayne Lee, Jim Gallagher, Claude Schlesinger, Jerry Gardiner, Lenny Whetsel, Roland Ladreyt, Joe Labarriere, and Jairo Leon, who all contributed to this book.

I thank Johnny Frederic, Tommy Tizzard, and Jim Gallagher, who helped coordinate the Fraternal Order of Police Hurricane Katrina relief efforts. I thank my many friends in the Fraternal Order of Police nationwide, who provided aid to their counterparts in the Gulf South during our darkest hour. They responded with supplies, manpower, understanding, and compassion. I thank St. Charles Parish Sheriff Greg Champagne, Chief Deputy Joseph Cardella and the residents of St. Charles Parish for affording me an opportunity to be part of the Hurricane Katrina Response. I also wish to thank Denise Pritchard and Alice Champagne, who graciously agreed to spend countless hours correcting my English and miserable spelling.

And finally, to my wife, Gail, who had to live this event twice: once when Hurricane Katrina struck, and again during the writing of this book. Her encouragement kept me focused and her support keeps me moving forward.

Preface

URGENT - WEATHER MESSAGE
NATIONAL WEATHER SERVICE NEW ORLEANS, LA
1011 AM CDT SUN AUG 28 2005

...DEVASTATING DAMAGE EXPECTED...

HURRICANE KATRINA...A MOST POWERFUL HURRICANE WITH UNPRECEDENTED STRENGTH... RIVALING THE INTENSITY OF HURRICANE CAMILLE OF 1969.

MOST OF THE AREA WILL BE UNINHABITABLE FOR WEEKS...PERHAPS LONGER. AT LEAST ONE HALF OF WELL-CONSTRUCTED HOMES WILL HAVE ROOF AND WALL FAILURE. ALL GABLED ROOFS WILL FAIL...LEAVING THOSE HOMES SEVERELY DAMAGED OR DESTROYED.

THE MAJORITY OF INDUSTRIAL BUILDINGS WILL BECOME NON-FUNCTIONAL. PARTIAL TO COMPLETE WALL AND ROOF FAILURE IS EXPECTED. ALL WOOD-FRAMED LOW-RISING APARTMENT BUILDINGS WILL BE DESTROYED. CONCRETE BLOCK LOW-RISE APARTMENTS WILL SUSTAIN MAJOR DAMAGE... INCLUDING SOME WALL AND ROOF FAILURE.

HIGH-RISE OFFICE AND APARTMENT BUILDINGS WILL SWAY DANGEROUSLY... A FEW TO THE POINT OF TOTAL COLLAPSE. ALL WINDOWS WILL BLOW OUT.

AIRBORNE DEBRIS WILL BE WIDESPREAD...AND
MAY INCLUDE HEAVY ITEMS SUCH AS HOUSEHOLD
APPLIANCES AND EVEN LIGHT VEHICLES. SPORT
UTILITY VEHICLES AND LIGHT TRUCKS WILL
BE MOVED. THE BLOWN DEBRIS WILL CREATE
ADDITIONAL DESTRUCTION. PERSONS...PETS...
AND LIVESTOCK EXPOSED TO THE WINDS WILL
FACE CERTAIN DEATH IF STRUCK.

POWER OUTAGES WILL LAST FOR WEEKS...AS MOST
POWER POLES WILL BE DOWN AND TRANSFORMERS
DESTROYED. WATER SHORTAGES WILL MAKE HUMAN
SUFFERING INCREDIBLE BY MODERN STANDARDS.

THE VAST MAJORITY OF NATIVE TREES WILL BE
SNAPPED OR UPROOTED. ONLY THE HEARTIEST
WILL REMAIN STANDING...BUT BE TOTALLY
DEFOLIATED. FEW CROPS WILL REMAIN. LIVESTOCK
LEFT EXPOSED TO THE WINDS WILL BE KILLED.

AN INLAND HURRICANE WIND WARNING IS ISSUED
WHEN SUSTAINED WINDS NEAR HURRICANE FORCE...
OR FREQUENT GUSTS AT OR ABOVE HURRICANE
FORCE...ARE CERTAIN WITHIN THE NEXT 12 TO
24 HOURS.

ONCE TROPICAL STORM AND HURRICANE FORCE
WINDS ONSET...DO NOT VENTURE OUTSIDE!

Introduction

Causing extensive damage in the southern portions of Louisiana, Mississippi, and Alabama on August 29, 2005, Hurricane Katrina was the costliest and one of the deadliest hurricanes in American history. While the storm's destructive winds and invasive tidal surge took over 1,450 lives with an estimated 200 people still believed missing, and caused catastrophic damage, the elements of this disaster were in place long before Hurricane Katrina made landfall. The lack of planning and prompt action at all levels of government created the perfect atmosphere for a total breakdown in society.

Nearly every local television and radio station was knocked off the air. Telephone and radio communications went dead. Trying to escape rising floodwaters, tens of thousands of people were stranded on rooftops. Looting and lawlessness were rampant in the streets. With all of this, elected officials of the rapidly flooding City of New Orleans and state emergency planners were trying to develop a plan of action at the height of the disaster, with virtually no way to communicate. They did so while standing in floodwater that was chest deep and rising.

Immersed in floodwaters and uncertainty, while receiving exaggerated news reports, the senses of first responders were challenged at every turn. Chest Deep and Rising tells of a nightmare that lasted 16 intense days, as seen through the eyes of law enforcement officers throughout the entire New Orleans metropolitan area. It is a story of bravery, heroic acts, and selfless devotion by America's first responders during a time when local, state, and federal services failed to adequately support these heroes. It was a time when the law enforcement community took charge and supported their counterparts with supplies and manpower. This is the story of but a few of the many heroes of Hurricane Katrina who made the difference at a time when the future seemed out of reach.

Hopefully, this book will inspire others to share their Hurricane Katrina experiences.

Foreword

Hanging on the wall of my office in the St. Charles Sheriff's Office's Special Services building, next to the Parish Courthouse in Hahnville, Louisiana, are several old photographs and newspaper articles depicting the rich and diverse history of St. Charles Parish. Among these keepsakes are early photographs of the towns of Norco and Good Hope, early local law enforcement figures, and a framed front-page copy of the St. Charles Herald newspaper's September 16, 1965 issue. The newspaper article has hung there for years, as a constant reminder of the past challenges St. Charles Parish has faced. More importantly, it stands as a reminder that the more things change, the more they stay the same.

The headline reads, "PARISH SURVIVES BETSY, BUT RECOVERY WILL TAKE MONTHS." Depicted are three compelling photos documenting the devastation caused by Hurricane Betsy, which struck the Louisiana coast on September 9, 1965. One photo is of downed power lines, snapped like matchsticks by 120 mph winds. The second photo is of the Destrehan-Luling Ferry, a large vessel capable of transporting vehicles across the swift currents of the Mississippi River, as it made its way down the final leg of a journey to the Gulf of Mexico. The Ferry was resting on dry ground. A tidal surge had pushed it outside the riverbank before the water receded. The third is a photo of Dr. John Clayton's mansion ablaze, the result of a candle left burning as the local physician rushed his dying wife to a hospital during the height of Hurricane Betsy's brutal winds. Each photo emphasizes the indiscriminate, destructive forces of nature, our vulnerability along the Gulf South, and Mother Nature's ability to forever change lives.

Living in southeast Louisiana, I fully understood our weaknesses, going all the way back to my first memories. As a four-year-old child living in Norco, a quiet little industrial town located in St. Charles Parish, Louisiana's equivalent of counties, located just 20 miles west of the City of New Orleans, I recall Hurricane Betsy and all the storm preparations going on around me. Although I didn't understand what was about to happen, I do remember the fear and concern felt by those who I thought were fearless.

I vividly remember being awakened at nighttime to experience the eye of the storm. I recall being terrified as my father opened the back door of our modest single-story home, the only protection that stood between me and the very thing my whole family feared. In my mind, an open door would let Betsy inside our home, and I wanted none of that. As we all walked outside, I recall staring up into the sky and seeing millions of stars, thanks to power outages that kept the nearby oil refinery lights from distorting the sky overhead. I also remember a very calm breeze. The whole experience left me confused as I tried, with the reasoning of a four-year-old, to make sense of the fear of hurricanes. My confusion only grew greater in the days that followed, as the damage to my very small world became apparent.

Nearby New Orleans suffered a devastating blow as levees gave way and flooded parts of the city. Many found refuge in their attics, where some were trapped and drowned. From that point on, nearly every attic in the region was equipped with a hatchet to hack a way out if needed. This practice proved invaluable years later for many Hurricane Katrina victims trapped in their attics.

Hurricane Betsy and the many storms that threatened the region thereafter have caused me to develop a fascination and profound respect for the powerful forces of Mother Nature. I have since witnessed many storms, some with tremendous challenges, but more often, only inconveniences that became the nightmares of others as the New Orleans metro area was spared. On August 29, 2005, our luck ran out.

As Hurricane Katrina approached, one and a half million people were told to evacuate southeast Louisiana, southern Mississippi and southern Alabama, with thousands of emergency workers left behind to protect life and property. As first responders, their assignment was to protect life and property during extraordinary conditions. Hurricane Katrina forever changed our nation. For those who called this region their home, our world would never be the same. Immersed in floodwaters and uncertainty, receiving exaggerated news reports, confused and dazed, senses challenged at every corner, each survivor has a story to tell. Finding the right words to explain this brief period of time is often difficult.

This story conveys a moment when the future seemed out of reach, and out of control. It was a time when our world collapsed all around us. It was a time of ever-changing challenges, unspeakable horrors, and survival. Equally important, it was a time of bravery, heroic acts, and selfless devotion by America's first responders. Looking back at the events before, during, and after what has become known as the worst natural disaster in American history, there are many lessons to learn about the resiliency of local law enforcement and a greater need for pre-planning.

For those who stayed, it was a nightmare that lasted 16 intense days, ending only with the reality that our lives and priorities had forever changed as we began the long, painful task of rebuilding. One and half a million people, just like me, have their own story to tell of how Hurricane Katrina changed them. This is my story.

The New Orleans Area

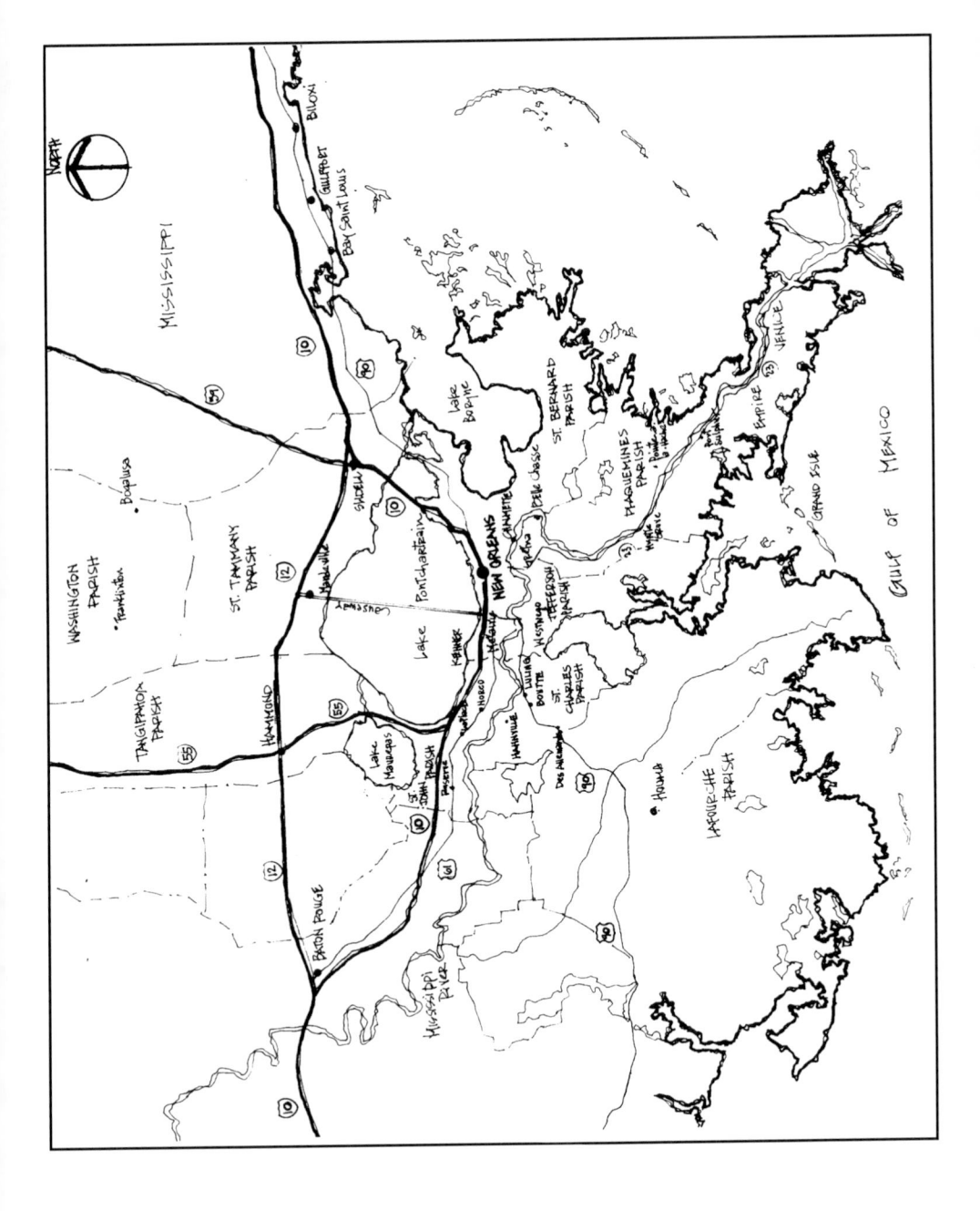

Downtown New Orleans

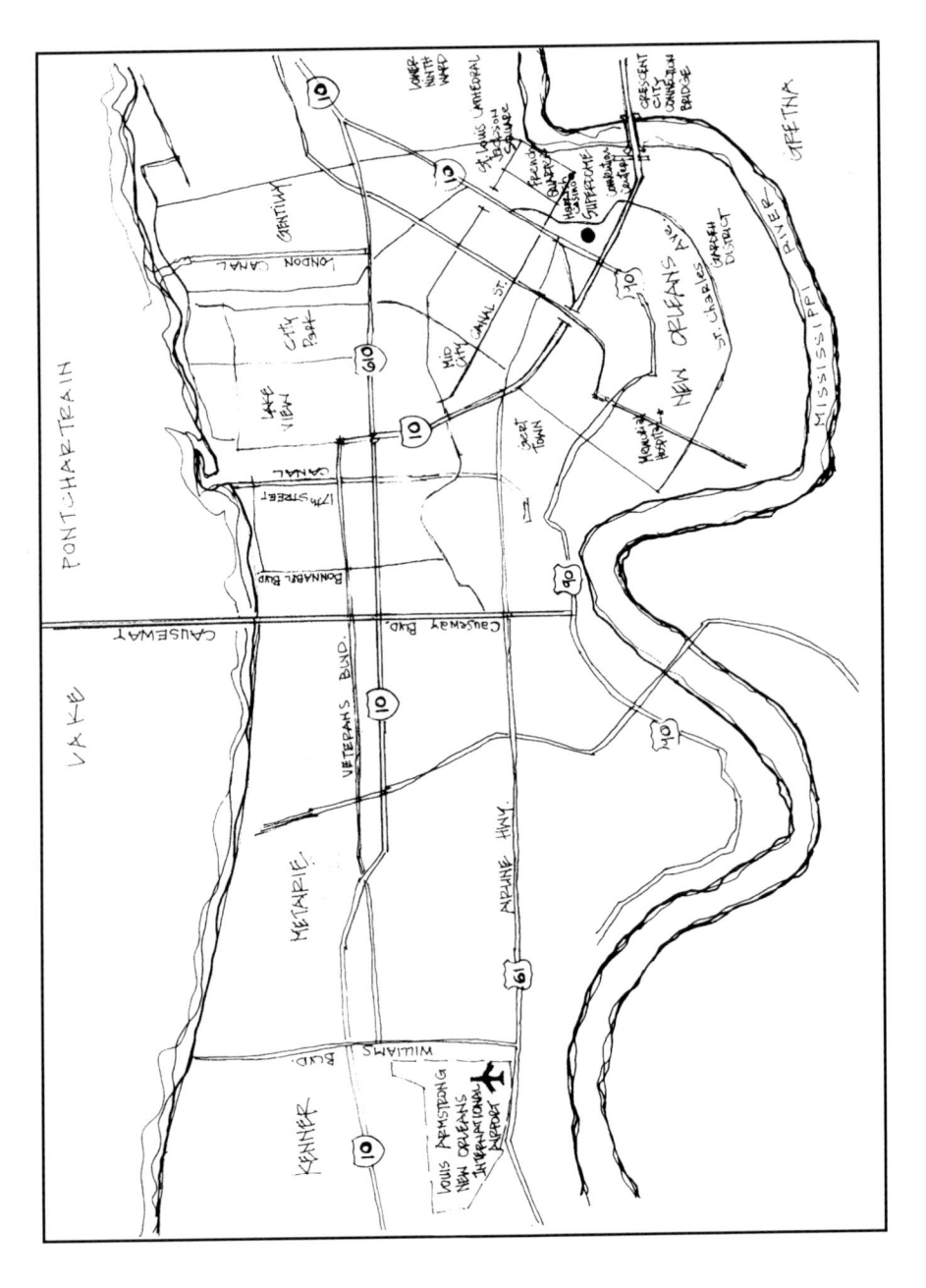

PART ONE

Day One
Friday, August 26, 2005

Weekend Plans Take an Unexpected Turn

With blue skies and the usual brutal, humid summertime temperatures, which we in the south have learned to tolerate but have never really gotten used to, Friday, August 26, 2005 was pretty much like any other summer day. During the morning news, the weather forecasters gave an update on Hurricane Katrina, then a minimal hurricane churning in the Atlantic with sights set on landfall on the southern Florida coastline. The storm was forecast to venture into the warm waters of the Gulf of Mexico, where she was to regain strength and make a second landfall in the panhandle of Florida near Pensacola (Hurricane Katrina would probably be a Category 2 storm on the Saffir-Simpson Hurricane Scale, with winds ranging between 96 and 110 miles per hour). The forecast was basically unchanged. This same prediction had been repeated for several days.

Given that Pensacola was still trying to recover from Hurricane Ivan, which had crippled that area some 11 months earlier, in addition to the four destructive storms that had pelted the Florida coast during the unusually active 2004 hurricane season, I couldn't help thinking that those "poor Floridians" just couldn't catch a break.

All around the St. Charles Parish Sheriff's Office, where I have worked since 1984, plans were being made for what was expected to be a pleasant weekend with clear skies and a light breeze, compliments of Hurricane Katrina and her anticipated landfall 300 miles and three states over to our east.

For me, it was a slower-paced life than I had been accustomed to. In fact, this was a time in my life to which I had looked forward with great anticipation. By mid-August 2005, and all within an eight-week period, my daughter, Thyme, had graduated from Louisiana State University and my department had successfully campaigned for a tax election dedicated to Sheriff's Office employee salaries. The National Fraternal Order of Police Conference, attended by 7,000 guests, which I had played a significant role in hosting, had just concluded successfully; and best of all, my son, Patrick, Jr., had just returned safely from a tour of duty in Iraq. All was right with my world. My wife, Gail, and I had our sights set on an upcoming trip to Las Vegas. We were really enjoying the prospect of a simpler life.

This Friday morning gave no cause for concern; in fact, it was about as typical as they get. After the normal routine of a summer Friday, returning calls and attending meetings, I geared up for the weekend and readied myself for an extra duty detail that evening at Hahnville High School, where I would be supervising 35 deputies and providing security at a large, popular high school football game.

A habit I had developed during hurricane season was to monitor storm activity and relay it to my coworkers who passed by my office, looking for updates. There are a few websites I routinely check and compare as I develop my tropical storm "hunch." Friday morning gave no reason for concern, although that was about to change. I printed out an updated hurricane report, and for the first time, I realized that the Hurricane Katrina forecast had shifted further west. I immediately looked at the activities of the offshore production platforms in the Gulf of Mexico to see what their forecasts were saying.

The national weather services, as well as local forecasters, have their greatest confidence in predicting forces of nature no more than 72 hours in advance. As such, they are guarded in releasing information beyond that point. In an industry where hours could cost millions of dollars in revenue, the offshore production companies employ private weather services for more advanced warning. The discussions of these weather services gave cause for considerable concern. I relayed my concern to my boss, Chief Deputy Joseph Cardella, and was told that should the forecast continue to drift further west, he would call a staff meeting to institute our Hurricane Plan.

As I left the office for my security detail, I asked coworkers in my building to disconnect their computers to protect the equipment in case of a power surge. Although the landfall prediction was near the Florida and Alabama state line at that time, further movement west would influence the weather in the New Orleans metro area. I had also informed non-enforcement staff that should the track of the storm continue to drift to the west, they needed to monitor the government access cable channel for instructions about possible public office closures on Monday.

At the football game, there was a definite rumble of conversation among the vast majority of those in attendance. News was spreading fast to those who had no idea that the storm's path had shifted west. Many had watched evening news reports emphasizing Louisiana Governor Kathleen Blanco's emergency declaration for all of Louisiana. Throughout the game, I monitored forecast reports from offshore production companies on my cell phone screen, and became more and more concerned that this could be the storm we in Louisiana had always feared. Frequent announcements were made from the press box: "The St. Charles Parish School Board is monitoring the progress of Hurricane Katrina. Residents should tune into local television and radio stations for updates."

Throughout the evening, my phone rang continuously with people asking questions, providing updates, seeking my thoughts on what the storm track change might bring. I was notified that there would be a Sheriff's Office staff meeting at 10:00 A.M. at the Courthouse. By the time the security detail ended, I had placed all my personnel on standby, told them to get their personal affairs in order as soon as possible, and to be prepared to report to duty when called. I had done the same, calling my wife and daughters to advise them to start securing everything in the yard and to prepare to evacuate in the morning. This is a drill my family is very much accustomed to and has practiced many times during my 22 years in law enforcement. Even the glancing blow of a minimal storm places tremendous demands on my agency and family, since St. Charles Parish is host to several evacuation routes.

I called my sister, Cindy, who works for the Louisiana Department of Wildlife and Fisheries at a research station in Grand Isle, and surprised her with the information about Hurricane Katrina. Cindy lives in my family vacation home, located on Louisiana's only inhabited barrier island. I gave her instructions on preparing the property for the storm and advised her to evacuate north as soon as she could, to beat what was sure to be heavy traffic.

When I returned home, around 11:00 P.M., I was very pleased with the preparations taken by my family and knew they understood just how serious the threat was. In addition to everything being secured, even a 50-pound Japanese pagoda lantern made of concrete had been removed from our oriental garden and placed in the garage for safekeeping. Everyone in the house was concerned and knew that first thing in the morning, they would leave for the in-laws' home in Baton Rouge, and possibly further north if the situation warranted.

Day Two
Saturday, August 27, 2005

Evacuation Begins

Unable to sleep, I stared endlessly at the alarm clock, fighting the urge to turn on the television to get an update on the storm track. Around 5:00 A.M., I gave in and turned on the Weather Channel, only to learn that adjustments in the previous storm track by the weather service were now showing the Louisiana and Mississippi state line as the projected landfall site of a storm that had exploded into a massive hurricane. This new track put the landfall less than 50 miles east of my home. Making last-minute preparations and getting the family ready for their departure, I watched my wife and girls walk around the house in a daze. I knew what they were thinking; I caught myself doing the same. Having just remodeled our home after a flood caused by a freak thunderstorm that dumped 18 inches of rain in a few short hours over my town only 16 months earlier, I knew that Katrina had the power to destroy all the hard work we had endured to put our home back together. As I left the house for my meeting, my family left for Baton Rouge with an uncertain return date. We all sensed this time would be different. Hurricane Katrina was quickly making it known that she would not be like other weather systems. We knew it might be some time before we saw each other again.

Before going to the Sheriff's Office meeting, I dropped in on the staff meeting in the St. Charles Parish Emergency Operations Center, located in the basement of the Courthouse. Given our high water table, it is one of only four basements I know of in St. Charles Parish. Around the department, many of us called it the "Dungeon of Doom." In the meeting room, a large screen serves as the backdrop of meetings, on which computer-generated worst-case scenario storms are routinely shown. Called the SLOSH (Sea, Lake, and Overland Surges from Hurricanes) Model, the National Weather Service developed this system to aid emergency planners by forecasting amazingly accurate storm surge heights from tropical systems all along the United States' East and Gulf coastlines, and certain territories of the US. The model generates a "hazard analysis" for coastal hurricane evacuation planning. After examining our vulnerability, as real storm paths from our past were replaced with make-believe storms with slightly different impact locations, well, the message certainly hit home. There is no complacency in St. Charles Parish; we know our vulnerabilities and make it part of our planning at nearly every meeting.

At 9:00 A.M., St. Charles Parish President Albert Laque called for a mandatory evacuation of St. Charles Parish and declared a state of emergency, setting into motion a host of events that mandated action by various public and private agencies and businesses. With a large concentration of petrochemical plants calling St. Charles Parish their home, each initiated the shutdown procedures and activated their own Hurricane Plans. The Emergency Operations Center was abuzz with activity as people from all branches of local government filed in and out, readying their hurricane preparations—a task that was almost second nature, given the number of times we have enacted this plan in St. Charles Parish in the past 20 or so years. With the exception of Hurricane Juan in 1985, which caused considerable flooding in St. Charles Parish, we had been fortunate enough to walk away, counting our blessings as these storms spared our region. At the Emergency Operation Center, I got the latest on the National Weather Service predictions from Emergency Operations Director Tab Troxler, and also viewed the computer-generated scenarios Hurricane Katrina could provide. This time we knew the threat was real, but hoped that this, too, would be a drill.

Lori Duplessis, Coordinator of a senior citizen program in St. Charles Parish, saw the news reports and drove to the St. Charles Emergency Operations Center to call senior citizens who she knew had special needs, and to offer assistance in their storm preparations. She commented on the high number of seniors she had spoken with who were unaware of the hurricane threat. They all had the impression, from earlier news reports, that the storm was going to impact Florida. Dedicated to her job, she had mixed feelings about evacuating. Her position in the Sheriff's Office is classified as non-enforcement. As such, she finished making her calls and reluctantly evacuated.

At the Sheriff's Office staff meeting, the mood was somewhat excited. Among St. Charles Parish governmental agencies, we all know our weaknesses, our vulnerability and, more importantly, our challenges. Years of taking these threats seriously have, on occasion, been the cause of criticism accusing us of over-reacting. Nonetheless, it is criticism we are prepared to receive, as the alternative means disaster. A year earlier, a group of Sheriff's Office members had visited Escambia County Sheriff's Office in Florida and learned firsthand what challenges faced that agency in the wake of Hurricane Ivan. It was lessons learned through that experience that, we hoped, would better prepare us for Hurricane Katrina.

One by one, we went around the table, explaining our responsibilities in the Hurricane Plan. Each detailed the steps they had taken and activities underway, and preparations for evacuation. We received directions from the St. Charles Parish Sheriff, Greg Champagne, and Chief Deputy Joseph Cardella, aimed at coordinating each division's efforts. For the first time, however, we found ourselves dealing with an issue we had never expected. Some members of the department were resigning. The tension caused by sending spouses and family away alone, and the fear of staying for what was beginning to be referred to as a "super hurricane" quickly became too much for some to handle. This was to be a dilemma that would resurface throughout the storm and its aftermath.

As Commander of the Special Services Division, my Hurricane Plan responsibility is the coordination of media relations and police presence at evacuation shelters. However, Hurricane Katrina would bring a different type of demand. She had grown in intensity to the extent that the St. Charles Parish Hospital had initiated plans to evacuate all patients north, to Desoto Regional Medical Center in Mansfield, LA, away from the threat of potential flooding. In addition, there would be no local shelters in St. Charles Parish for the general public. My new duties were to arrange for law enforcement escorts from the hospital to North Louisiana and to assign personnel to the evacuated hospital, which would serve as a police shelter and as a location where people refusing to evacuate would likely seek out as a shelter of last resort. I was also given the task of arranging a law enforcement shelter on the east bank of the Mississippi River, for deputies to ride out the storm.

Traffic quickly started to increase on the main arteries. St. Charles Sheriff's Office personnel were doubled up and placed on 12-hour rotating shifts. Checkpoints were established to maintain a constant flow of traffic, with much of the southern portion of Louisiana having to flow through St. Charles Parish. By an order of Governor Blanco, Contra Flow was instituted at 4:00 P.M. Contra Flow calls for the closure of the inbound lanes on Interstates 10, 55, and 59, and the redirection of all lanes as outflow to allow maximum flow from the region. Even with these actions, tested in past storms, traffic movement slowed to a snail's pace. A normal trip from New Orleans to Baton Rouge would take about an hour, on a good day; with the evacuation of 1.2 million people in the southeast region of Louisiana, this trip could take eight hours or more.

Listening to local talk/news WWL Radio during the evacuation, I heard caller after caller telephone in to complain about the slow pace of the evacuation progress. Many, however, complimented the St. Charles Parish Sheriff's Office for having deputies positioned at regular intervals along main traffic arteries and cycling traffic lights to keep traffic flowing. Unfortunately, not every jurisdiction did the same. A stoplight 30 miles away would often influence the flow of traffic in St. Charles Parish.

Throughout the day, with the assistance of St. Charles Sheriff's Office Sergeants Warren Lebeauf, Dwayne LaGrange, and Burley McCarter, all three assigned to the Special Services Division, we gathered supplies and made the necessary scheduling assignments and arrangements for the shelters to be equipped with the materials and equipment needed for an extended stay. To prepare for a response to members after the storm, I contacted Louisiana Fraternal Order of Police Director of Member Services Johnny Frederic, Vice-President Tommy

Tizzard and other board members; to discuss the role the organization would play immediately following the storm.

After 32 years as a member of the Jefferson Parish Sheriff's Office, Tommy Tizzard had retired at the rank of Lieutenant and gone to work in corporate security for a New Orleans company. Given the lack of hotel rooms available outside the affected areas, he, his brothers, and their families all evacuated their Jefferson Parish homes to the Louisiana State Fraternal Order of Police office, where they set up a temporary shelter. This office would be the Tizzard family compound for several weeks.

Johnny Frederic is a retired Sergeant with the Gonzales Police Department; he retired after 26 years in uniform and immediately went to work for the Fraternal Order of Police. Frederic resides in the community of St. Amant, Louisiana, 50 miles west of New Orleans, with his wife, Virginia, and daughter, Samantha. Johnny was on his way to purchase a generator for his home from a hardware store in Gonzales, and called to see if I wanted him to purchase one for me. I said, "Yes," and wondered if it was to be for nothing. We had had many close calls, but this one could be different. A half hour later, he called back, laughing, and said, "Forget about it." He had passed by the hardware store, and they were sold out of generators. Frederic made call after call to other stores and received the same response. Feeling like I had just saved $840, I thought nothing of it and went about my business. Fifteen minutes later, Frederic called again and said he was traveling on the Interstate, following a trailer loaded full of generators, and was going to follow them to wherever they were going and buy two of them. A couple of hours later, he showed up at my home with a 5400-watt generator. Later, I would come to realize that this was perhaps the best $840 I have ever spent.

Not certain how Hurricane Katrina would impact our ability to move about the parish, several law enforcement shelters were set up at various locations, mostly as guests at stations of local volunteer fire departments. The two shelters I was responsible for were the St. Charles Parish Hospital on the west bank and Harry Hurst Middle School on the east bank of the Mississippi River. Both shelters were to become operational by noon on Sunday.

At 4:00 P.M., I attended the evening briefing at the St. Charles Emergency Operations Center, where I got an update and watched more computer-generated scenarios. Checking my favorite Internet storm sites, I entered the zip code of my hometown of Norco into a wind-velocity generator, and learned that the projected landfall site forecasted sustained winds of 150 mph at the height of the storm. This wind speed crosses a threshold where virtually all structure failure occurs.

By 5:00 P.M., New Orleans Mayor, Ray Nagin, with Governor Blanco at his side, declared a state of emergency in the City of New Orleans, and issued a voluntary evacuation order for his city. He stopped short of a full evacuation order, saying he was having his legal team determine if he could order a mandatory evacuation without exposing the city to legal liability for the closure of hotels and other businesses. Mandatory evacuations are not new to southeast Louisiana residents. Other jurisdictions, including St. Charles Parish, call for mandatory evacuations frequently, due to their vulnerability to tidal surges. Never has this exposed the parish to legal liability. Even more, with the SLOSH Model available to every emergency planner and its forecasted tidal surge, it was hard to understand why New Orleans Emergency planners were delaying such an important decision.

That evening, I returned to my empty home and closed the storm shutters my son and I had built two years earlier, but had never had the opportunity to use. The neighborhood had begun to look like a ghost town, as most residents heeded the calls for evacuation. Walking through my home, absent of any outside light, the realization struck me that it might not survive Hurricane Katrina.

I spent most of the evening talking to family and friends on the phone, speculating on future events and making plans to reunite after the storm. One call came from my sister, Cindy, around 9:00 P.M. She was still packing to leave Grand Isle. The road to this island often washes out during storms. I was a little harsh with her on the phone; she needed to get off the island soon, or she could be trapped there.

By 10:00 P.M. that same night, after a call from National Hurricane Center Director Max Mayfield, Mayor Nagin appeared on four local television stations, strongly encouraging New Orleans residents to evacuate, but again he stopped short of declaring a mandatory evacuation. His hesitation in making such a crucial decision continued to waste valuable time.

Before turning in for the night, I walked around outside my home and met neighbors who were doing the same. I explained the SLOSH models forecast shown at the St. Charles Emergency Operations Center, what the scenarios could cause, and encouraged them all to leave. I gave them my cell number for reports on their property after the storm. One of the possibilities the SLOSH Model prediction suggested was a tidal surge that was higher than the levee protecting the east bank of St. Charles Parish from such tidal surges.

Again, I had a sleepless night.

Day Three
Sunday, August 28, 2005

Preparations Intensify

Sunday, August 28 started just as it had the day before, with the weather forecast at 5:00 A.M., only this time, the westward movement had ended and seemed to lock in on a landfall in my general area. Tropical force winds were expected to begin in less than 10 hours. All morning, I received calls from Fraternal Order of Police friends all across the country, expressing concern, pledging support, and offering well wishes. I gathered a few supplies, elevated my generator in case my home flooded again, and packed my police car with items intended to sustain me for a few days. As I walked out of my home, I stopped to talk to more neighbors and encouraged them to evacuate.

I attended the 9:00 A.M. briefing at the Emergency Operations Center and got the latest news, complete with a computer-generated forecast that demonstrated the potential flooding based on the more precise storm track. Each variation in landfall could cause different areas to flood. The predictions were frightening.

With the Hurricane Plan in full effect, our response took on the appearance of preparing for war. Everyone swung into action, trying to beat the clock. Local nursing homes had completed their evacuations, and stockpiles of food, supplies, equipment, and sandbags were being placed at strategic locations for use after the storm. There was a great deal of discussion about some of the staging areas and their ability to survive damage caused by such a powerful storm. The debate was as fierce as the sense of urgency.

At the 10:00 A.M. Sheriff's Office staff meeting, a full review of action was underway, and planning for an after-event response began to take shape. At the same time, New Orleans Mayor Ray Nagin ordered the first-ever mandatory evacuation of the City of New Orleans, an action that would certainly increase traffic flow through St. Charles Parish. With 300 St. Charles Sheriff's Office enforcement personnel assigned various duties, the evacuation continued, with a last-minute surge occurring as many accepted the realization that this was going to be "the big one."

Major Sam Zinna, Major John Cornwell, Captain Jon Walsdorf, and Captain Fred Oubre were assigned to the St. Charles Emergency Operations Center as law enforcement coordinators. Major John Nowak reported that the correctional facility had hunkered down. Inmates had filled sandbags and fortified the 800-bed facility. Lieutenant Wayne Lee explained the precautions to protect the department's information systems. Crime Scene was assigned to food preparation and distribution. Criminal and Special Investigations joined patrols, manning traffic checkpoints and increasing patrols. Captain Craig Petit reported that double shifts were operational in the Communications Center, with an employee shelter having been established. I explained the shelter preparations and the hospital's evacuation progress. All enforcement personnel and communications operators were either on duty or assigned to the opposite shift. All non-essential personnel had been ordered to evacuate.

If anyone still had doubts about the intensity of Hurricane Katrina, the National Weather Service's special advisory, issued at 10:11 A.M., should have convinced them otherwise. The report read:

URGENT WEATHER MESSAGE

NATIONAL WEATHER SERVICE NEW ORLEANS, LA

1011 AM CDT SUN AUG 28 2005

...DEVASTATING DAMAGE EXPECTED...

HURRICANE KATRINA...A MOST POWERFUL HURRICANE WITH UNPRECEDENTED STRENGTH...RIVALING THE INTENSITY OF HURRICANE CAMILLE OF 1969.

MOST OF THE AREA WILL BE UNINHABITABLE FOR WEEKS...PERHAPS LONGER. AT LEAST ONE HALF OF WELL-CONSTRUCTED HOMES WILL HAVE ROOF AND WALL FAILURE. ALL GABLED ROOFS WILL FAIL...LEAVING THOSE HOMES SEVERELY DAMAGED OR DESTROYED.

THE MAJORITY OF INDUSTRIAL BUILDINGS WILL BECOME NON-FUNCTIONAL. PARTIAL TO COMPLETE WALL AND ROOF FAILURE IS EXPECTED. ALL WOOD-FRAMED LOW-RISING APARTMENT BUILDINGS WILL BE DESTROYED. CONCRETE BLOCK LOW-RISE APARTMENTS WILL SUSTAIN MAJOR DAMAGE...INCLUDING SOME WALL AND ROOF FAILURE.

HIGH-RISE OFFICE AND APARTMENT BUILDINGS WILL SWAY DANGEROUSLY... A FEW TO THE POINT OF TOTAL COLLAPSE. ALL WINDOWS WILL BLOW OUT.

AIRBORNE DEBRIS WILL BE WIDESPREAD...AND MAY INCLUDE HEAVY ITEMS SUCH AS HOUSEHOLD APPLIANCES AND EVEN LIGHT VEHICLES. SPORT UTILITY VEHICLES AND LIGHT TRUCKS WILL BE MOVED. THE BLOWN DEBRIS WILL CREATE ADDITIONAL DESTRUCTION. PERSONS...PETS...AND LIVESTOCK EXPOSED TO THE WINDS WILL FACE CERTAIN DEATH IF STRUCK.

POWER OUTAGES WILL LAST FOR WEEKS...AS MOST POWER POLES WILL BE DOWN AND TRANSFORMERS DESTROYED. WATER SHORTAGES WILL MAKE HUMAN SUFFERING INCREDIBLE BY MODERN STANDARDS.

THE VAST MAJORITY OF NATIVE TREES WILL BE SNAPPED OR UPROOTED. ONLY THE HEARTIEST WILL REMAIN STANDING...BUT BE TOTALLY DEFOLIATED. FEW CROPS WILL REMAIN. LIVESTOCK LEFT EXPOSED TO THE WINDS WILL BE KILLED.

AN INLAND HURRICANE WIND WARNING IS ISSUED WHEN SUSTAINED WINDS NEAR HURRICANE FORCE...OR FREQUENT GUSTS AT OR ABOVE HURRICANE FORCE...ARE CERTAIN WITHIN THE NEXT 12 TO 24 HOURS.

ONCE TROPICAL STORM AND HURRICANE FORCE WINDS ONSET...DO NOT VENTURE OUTSIDE!

Chest Deep and Rising:

As I was passing by my office to make a few calls, Lieutenant Pam Schmitt finally called in. Since Saturday morning I
had tried several times to call her cell phone and left messages.
A Victim's Assistance Officer in the Special Services Division,
she and Lieutenant Pam Negrotto, a Domestic Violence Officer
also in the Special Services Division, had both left Thursday to
join a friend attending a conference in Reno, Nevada. Due to
their busy schedules in Reno, they were unaware of the storm
threat and had just learned a hurricane was approaching the
Gulf South. They wanted to return home immediately. I told
them they should stay put, since the airport was already beginning to shut down. Even though they were in a city 2,400 miles
away, safe from the destructive forces of Hurricane Katrina, they
were miserable, knowing their coworkers were preparing for an
emergency and they were helpless to assist. My main reason
for calling Lieutenant Schmitt was to get her police vehicle.
She drove a marked Ford pick-up that would allow a little more
clearance should there be flooding. I retrieved the truck from
her home and parked it at Harry Hurst Middle School.

Harry Hurst Middle School was selected as an east
bank shelter for several reasons. It has a second story for verti-
cal evacuation should excessive flooding occur. It is on high
ground and is centrally located on the east bank, next to the
Hale Boggs Mississippi River Bridge, part of the Interstate
310 highway system that links the east and west banks of St.
Charles Parish. Generators and supplies were delivered. Two
days before, the halls had teemed with students ready for the
weekend break. Now the school's cafeteria and adjacent hallways began to resemble an army barracks, as deputies arrived
to stake claim to cots.

By Sunday evening, St. Charles Parish Hospital had
been closed to patient intake and stripped down to minimal

staffing levels, with only one patient who was deemed too frail to make the journey to North Louisiana. Most of the evacuated patients made it to their destination. With a misunderstanding of departure times, some of the patients were delayed and spent three days in a Special Needs shelter in Lafayette, Louisiana, before rejoining the others in Mansfield. Several Sheriff's Office employees were assigned to report to the hospital as their shelter. Those working the day shift were to report prior to 10:00 P.M. on Sunday night, the likely time identified when the winds would make driving hazardous.

After attending another briefing in the St. Charles Emergency Operation Center, the reality of a direct hit was even more evident. Leaving the meeting, I drove by a young adult I knew who was sitting on the tailgate of his truck, talking on a cell phone. I stopped my car, walked over and asked him what he was doing. "Waiting to see where the storm will hit before deciding if I should leave or stay," he responded. With the images of the computer-generated storm surge fresh in my mind from the meeting only minutes before, I let out a string of expletives and insults directed at his youthful misunderstanding of what was about to happen. I told him to leave as I walked back to my police car. The tone of my voice was all he needed to convince him. He climbed into his truck and left immediately.

With the shelter at Harry Hurst taking shape, along with shelters at fire stations and the courthouse, I took some time to call Fraternal Order of Police leadership in the evacuated parishes and at the national level to further discuss the support network we were developing to assist our members during recovery. I spoke to Willie Patin, another member of the State and National Fraternal Order of Police boards. A retired New Orleans Police Officer and now Director of Security for an international natural resource company, Willie advised he would ride out the storm in the comfort of their twenty-three-story building across the street from the Louisiana Superdome. He had brought family members there with him.

As night fell, the winds began to increase from a steady breeze to a considerable gust that started to topple some trees and had already blown away part of the emergency room awning at the St. Charles Parish Hospital. The quickest way to cross the Mississippi River in St. Charles Parish is by using the Interstate 310 Hale Boggs Bridge. With travel lanes elevated nearly 180 feet above the Mississippi River and a cable suspension and support structure rising over 300 feet in the air, exposure to the elements makes crossing the bridge very challenging during high crosswinds.

Not wanting to find myself stranded on the west bank of the river when high winds forced the closure of the Hale Boggs Bridge, I made one last trip to St. Charles Parish Hospital to check on the deputies assigned to that location before returning to the east bank to ride out the storm. At the hospital, the mood was subdued; most there were old enough to remember Hurricane Betsy, nearly forty years earlier, and knew what was in store. An elderly couple that had not evacuated had arrived, hoping to get prescription medication before the storm came. We talked briefly and wished each other well.

Fear of the Unknown

Standing outside the hospital, near the emergency room entrance, I made another call to Colonel Charles Guey with the Plaquemines Parish Sheriff's Department. He has been a good friend for many years, and I was surprised when he answered; the volume of calls on cell towers was causing many dropped calls. Colonel Guey told me he was at the Port Sulphur Substation and 911 Communications Center, located halfway down the sliver of land protruding into the Gulf of Mexico that makes up the boot-like shape of Louisiana's outline. He advised they were experiencing gusts in excess of 70 miles an hour, and that he and Plaquemines Sheriff Jiff Hingle were locking up the Communications Center and preparing to travel further inland to Belle Chasse, where they would ride out the storm. Of all southeast Louisiana, Plaquemines Parish is the most vulnerable, and they knew it. Several members of his department had already abandoned their posts and evacuated with their families. We wished each other well and promised to call the next day to let each other know how we had fared the storm. This was a promise delayed for nine days.

After talking with Sergeant Pink Duckworth, the supervisor on duty at St. Charles Parish Hospital for the night shift, and Hospital Administrator Fred Martinez, I headed over the bridge for the last time that night. Pushed all over the roadway by increasing winds, I recalled a time several years earlier when I had crossed the bridge during a minimal storm and witnessed the violent swaying of the structure, caused by 80 mph winds. I wondered if the large structure would survive the direct hit of a Category 5 storm.

Arriving at Harry Hurst Middle School, I set up my cot in a corner of the cafeteria, against a door leading into the kitchen. With 50 deputies having done the same, most of them in their twenties and having never experienced a direct hit from a hurricane, it was a strange atmosphere. I directed almost all of them to drive to the elevated portion of Interstate 310, a quarter-mile from the school. There, two-thirds of the law enforcement vehicles were parked on the shoulder of the elevated roadway to protect them from potential flooding. Piling into a few of the vehicles, they headed back to the school for the night. There was a great deal of kidding and joking, but you could also sense the ever-present anxiety of the unknown.

Harry Hurst Middle School afforded a unique benefit that had been unknown when the site was selected as a shelter. The building blocked the brunt of the growing winds by means of the covered bus breezeway, affording an area to sit outside and watch the storm in relative safety. As I sat alone on a bench under the bus breezeway, watching the trees sway in the building wind, a young rookie deputy approached and asked what I thought was going to happen. I didn't want to alarm him, but I wanted to be honest. I reassured him that I felt comfortable our shelter would fare well and our safety was our first objective. I went on to explain that regardless of where the storm hit, our ability to move about would be hampered by downed power lines, trees, and debris blocking roads, and I expected we would be working double shifts for weeks until power was restored and residents were allowed to return. A look of disbelief covered his face as he questioned whether I really thought it would be that bad. He slowly and quietly walked to his cot and lay there in silence.

As time passed, there was an interesting atmosphere in the shelter. A handful of older officers were huddled around the television, watching the same weather advisories over and over. Others, much younger and having never witnessed anything higher than a minimal hurricane, sat telling jokes as they played cards. An even smaller number lay quietly on their cots, listening to the sound of the growing winds, either praying or reflecting on the past and the future. One older deputy, a self-proclaimed legend who seemed to have seen and done everything imaginable, boastfully entertained rookies with colorful descriptions of his alleged heroic actions during events of which I seemed to have a slightly different recollection. Nonetheless, he created a diversion from the reality that lurked in the Gulf of Mexico.

Lieutenant George Breedy stopped by the shelter for a few minutes, laid claim to an empty cot, and then asked me to take a ride with him to his home nearby so he could get his supplies. The winds were steadily increasing as we ventured to different parts of the east bank of St. Charles Parish for one last look before Hurricane Katrina rearranged it. The rain was off and on, but the winds were pretty consistent. I'm not sure of the actual wind speed at the time, but it clearly made driving a bit challenging, both due to being pushed by winds and traversing the downed trees and power lines that had started to cover the roadway.

Not long after our return to the school, an announcement across the police radio echoed throughout the school building. All personnel were ordered to report to their assigned shelters for the duration of the storm. One by one, the on-duty shift filed into the school, signed in, and shared their observations with those huddled around the television. Some joined the card game and others turned in for the night. A bit of good news was suggested by forecasters on the television; at least, something to hope for. Hurricane Katrina appeared to be decreasing in wind strength, to a Category 4 storm with winds ranging between 131 and 155 miles per hour, as she wobbled a bit eastward. Only time would tell if this was to be the case.

My cell phone rang a couple of times. My wife and kids had moved from my mother-in-law's home in Baton Rouge to my stepdaughter's home in Gonzales, information that I did not find comforting. Gonzales was only forty miles west of my location. Experiencing high winds, they had already lost power and were settled down for the night with eight people in the house. Another call came from my brother, Mike, who had evacuated to Lake Charles (located on the westernmost part of the state), to the home of my older brother, Gene. I was pleased to get his call, since the last time I had spoken to him, he was determined to ride out the storm in his Destrehan home. Our previous conversation had been pretty intense as I explained my views on his decision to stay. What he didn't know was that his wife, Marlene, had asked me to talk some sense into him, since she wanted to evacuate and he didn't. They made the trip and he was pretty upset about the travel time and traffic. He asked that I check his home after the storm and give him a call.

Around 1:00 A.M., a strong gust of wind blew a kitchen vent cover off the school's cafeteria roof. Rainwater began to pour into the kitchen area, but more importantly, the winds caused an eerie howl that seemed to be more pronounced near my cot. As the winds came and went, the pressure changes caused the doors and vent pipes to rattle. Not long after, the power failed and suddenly, the mood changed. Previously, it had been an almost festive atmosphere, joking, speculating. Now, as everyone sat in near-darkness broken only by a couple of flashlights, reality set in… it was as if Katrina had knocked on the door to announce her arrival. Corporal James Hebert, a School Resource Officer who is known by many nicknames, one of which is Inspector Gadget for his resourcefulness, went out and started the generators, charging a maze of extension cords he had arranged throughout the building earlier in the day. This provided some lighting, a large fan, and allowed the television to function. The sound of the generators muffled the sounds of the wind and vent howling. With few exceptions, everyone lay quietly on their cots, though I doubt anyone got much sleep.

Day Four
Monday, August 29, 2005

Katrina Arrives, and Boy, is She Mad!

As I lay on my cot, wide awake yet at the same time starting to feel fatigued, the effects from two and a half days of intense planning, uncertainty, and the lack of sleep began to set in. My phone rang at around 5:00 A.M. Chief Cardella, who was riding out the storm at the St. Charles Parish Courthouse, called to see how we were making out—or so he said. I suspect his true motive had to do more with his pleasure in describing how the roof of my office was flying away, piece by piece. It turned out that he and others were rating the wind gusts on a point system from one to five, with five being the furthest a part of my roof would land from the building. His call was amusing but, from the sounds of the increasing winds outside, his comment about the roof damage was not surprising.

Quietly I made my way through the school cafeteria, trying not to disturb anyone as I ventured out to the bus breezeway. Waiting for someone to be the first, others quickly joined me. I stopped by the television and got good news. Hurricane Katrina had indeed wobbled a little to the east as she prepared to make landfall. Although we all knew this was not good news for areas east of New Orleans, it suggested that St. Charles Parish would be spared the worst of the intense winds of the storm's eye wall.

As daylight arrived, so did sustained winds in excess of 100 mph, with gusts much higher. At 6:10 A.M., the eye wall of Hurricane Katrina, with 145 mph gusts, made initial landfall in Plaquemines Parish near Buras, LA. We all watched in amazement as the metal roofs of nearby homes and buildings were peeled off like paper and became missiles flying through the air. If they landed on a fence, the fence quickly collapsed. If they became entangled in power lines, the lines were ripped from the homes. Each gust announced its arrival by way of a roar, as treetops snapped in the distance, and became louder as the gust worked its way closer.

I tried to call my family, but cell service was jammed. We still had radio communications, but with power outages and antennas moved out of alignment, communications began to deteriorate rapidly. We sat quietly, watching in amazement and concern as Hurricane Katrina roared on for hours. Attempts to get updates from the television began to fade when the cable system went out. A makeshift antenna, crafted by Inspector Gadget, gave a distorted reception that allowed us to watch the updates, although the information was recycled. Any new information would have to wait until it was safe to venture outside to conduct assessments. With few exceptions, this would be the last television I would see for weeks.

Unknown to us at the time, Hurricane Katrina's storm surge had pushed water over the Industrial Canal levees east of New Orleans. Soon after, a barge 200 feet in length broke loose from its mooring and flowed through the breached floodwall. Flooding accelerated into parts of New Orleans and St. Bernard Parish. At 8:14 A.M., the National Weather Service, New Orleans office, issued a flash flood warning, stating there had been a levee breach. At. 9:00 A.M., the eye of Hurricane Katrina passed over the City of New Orleans, as six to eight feet of water covered New Orleans' Lower Ninth Ward.

At Harry Hurst Middle School, we sat and watched in astonishment as the forces of nature raged endlessly. We moved throughout the buildings to get different views. Portable classroom buildings collapsed, trees snapped or uprooted. It was an awesome sight.

Around noon, with sustained winds diminishing, news reports started rolling in that Hurricane Katrina had ripped two holes in the roof of the Louisiana Superdome. At that time, reports were that there were 10,000 people in the Superdome. That number would later prove to be much higher.

Time to Venture Outside

With the winds dying down, it was time to venture out to survey the damage. As downed power lines were blocking the main school entrance, Lieutenant Breedy and myself slipped out through a side gate. We first passed by his home, only blocks away, to learn that his house had fared well, but did have some roof and rain water damage. Travel was difficult, with trees and power lines down as far as the eye could see. The east wall of a two-story brick office of a local attorney had collapsed near the school, as had many smaller buildings. We were pleased to see that for the most part, flooding was minimal and structural damage, although widely visible, was far less than we had anticipated. The last-minute wobble to the east had spared us.

Within an hour, the day shift had been deployed and the tedious and time-consuming process of checking damaged structures for injured and making the roadways passable had commenced. With the lack of any major flooding, we were all feeling pretty good. We had expected the worst and so far, we found that we had fared far better than anticipated. Listening to radio reports, it was apparent that there was serious damage throughout the New Orleans area, but the levees in St. Charles Parish had held so far.

Although there was a great deal of street and residential flooding, it was caused by rainwater, not tidal surge. The worst part of any hurricane is not the winds: it is the tidal surge that arrives with such force that even the strongest of buildings can collapse. Listening to news reports on WWL Radio, one of the only local news stations still broadcasting in the New Orleans area, it was apparent that the threat wasn't over. By 2:00 P.M., New Orleans city officials confirmed that the 17th Street Canal Levee had also breached, flooding the residential Lakeview area.

I made my way to my home, using Lieutenant Schmitt's truck. Determined to get to my home, and blocked by downed utility poles on the roadway, I was forced to detour through standing water on the street. I knew I had made a poor decision to drive through such deep water, but stopping would flood the truck and result in a long walk in deep water. As I drove, I realized I was striking submerged debris, but I was more concerned with staying on the roadway. I eventually made it to my home, which was literally inches away from flooding. I pulled into my driveway and killed the engine, only to learn that the transmission linkage on the truck had disconnected, apparently from striking submerged debris. In gear, I couldn't restart the truck, and lying in the water to reattach it was not something I intended to do. Wading through water, I entered my home and was pleased to see I had fared quite well. Roof damage was the only thing apparent at that point, I called for Lieutenant Breedy who passed by and picked me up. Together, we proceeded to check on other officers' homes, as well as neighbors.

Levee breaches had caused widespread flooding in the City of New Orleans. Reports that levees had breached in Jefferson Parish also started to surface. Both the levees in Orleans and Jefferson Parishes are much higher than the levees in St. Charles Parish. The initial excitement that we had come through okay gave way to concern that our levee system would also fail, flooding the east bank of the parish. For the most part, the levees in St. Charles Parish were holding. One weak area showed signs of breaching in the St. Rose area, near the New Orleans International Airport runway, adjacent to railroad tracks. This caused some flooding in that portion of the parish before quick repairs by St. Charles Parish Public Works employees fortified the levee and held back the waters.

Visiting the St. Charles Emergency Operation Center, I learned that the conditions were indeed rapidly deteriorating in the City of New Orleans. People were stranded on rooftops, holding up signs and pleading for help.

With tropical storm conditions still battering the City of New Orleans, US Coast Guard helicopters responded from Air Stations in New Orleans, Houston, and the Aviation Training Center in Mobile. They descended on the devastated area, finding a city underwater. Many homes had been flattened by high winds; there were ruptured natural gas pipelines lines burning out of control; and tens of thousands of survivors were clinging to rooftops and calling for help. Helicopter crews immediately began hoisting survivors and delivering those recovered to the nearest dry land or highway overpasses.

Others were wading through floodwaters as they migrated to the Louisiana Superdome, a location identified during this and previous storms as a "shelter of last resort." The flooding would eventually cover 80% of the city. Communications were non-existent. The 504 Area Code switching center had flooded, knocking out the ability to call that area code. The 911 Communications Centers were out of service, as were almost all radio communications, due to repeater failures. Television stations had flooded, as well as most radio stations. Many would remain off the air for weeks. Hurricane Katrina had moved north and left the Gulf South ravaged. Her floodwaters, however, remained, and were pouring into the city at an alarming rate.

Orleans Parish Prison was one of the largest of its kind, typically holding between 6,000 and 8,000 people at any given time in its ten buildings. While the hardened buildings were designed to withstand the hurricane itself, when it came to flooding, it was just as vulnerable as the rest of the city. As floodwaters rushed into the City of New Orleans, water rose to seven feet deep in some of the jail's buildings.

With water rising, inmates on the first floor of some buildings were trapped in the cells, standing chest deep in floodwaters. Other areas of the prison were out of control, with inmates rioting. Officers on the scene were far outnumbered. Special Agents with the Louisiana Attorney General's Office and officers with the Louisiana Department of Corrections responded to assist an overwhelmed Orleans Parish Criminal Sheriff's Office. An inventory of every incarcerated person at the facility was needed to assist in the evacuation. As officers started a generator at the Orleans Parish Criminal Sheriff's building to power the agency's main computer and copy an inventory list of inmates, they came under sniper fire.

Treading water and under the constant threat of sniper fire, the officers escorted approximately 7,000 Orleans Parish Prison inmates to a nearby elevated roadway, where they sat in the baking sun with armed guards watching over them until buses could take them to other correctional facilities throughout the state. This evacuation would eventually take three full days to complete.

While the American Red Cross seemed to understand the magnitude of what had occurred in the Gulf South, FEMA Director Michael Brown did not. Brown issued a press release urging emergency services personnel not to respond to the Gulf South unless requested to do so by FEMA. The American Red Cross, on the other hand, understood the level of the devastation and announced that it was launching the largest mobilization of resources in its history. FEMA, still fumbling to get a handle on the enormity of the event, encouraged the public to donate to the Red Cross and private organizations involved in the relief efforts.

That night, fatigued and exhausted, I slept in my home. I couldn't help feeling guilty doing so. I knew thousands had just become homeless, and many were fighting for their lives.

Day Five
Tuesday, August 30, 2005

A Never-ending, Ever-changing Challenge

With intense heat settling in over the region, Tuesday brought with it many challenges. The first was the lack of fuel. Emergency vehicles were running out of gas. With power outages and closed roadways, simple things became increasing difficult. Jackie Bee Corporation, a Phillips 66 supplier in St. Charles Parish, set up a generator at their shop and offered fuel to emergency personnel. Although a trip to get fuel meant a long wait in an even longer line, the fuel problem was solved! Returning home, with the help of Reserve Deputy Patrick Beard, we connected the generator power into my home's electrical panel and pulled the meter to prevent it from charging the downed power lines in my neighborhood. I installed a small 110-volt window air conditioner in the window of my living room with the intent of sleeping on the sofa that night, and I left the generator running to cool off the large room.

Floodwaters continued to pour unchecked into New Orleans. Large sandbags were being dropped by military helicopter into the breaches, only to be washed away by the intense current of water making its way into the city. Reports of widespread looting began to surface. From the Superdome, unbelievable reports of violence were emerging. Days later, many of these reports would be proven either false or exaggerated, but it didn't matter. The inability to communicate and verify rumors led to incorrect information being reported as fact. In this type of environment, perception is reality, and reality wasn't a pretty sight for those in the Gulf South. Only complicating matters, reports stated that as much as 60% of the New Orleans Police Force had abandoned their posts. Having many friends in that department, I knew this had to be an exaggeration, but being widely publicized, exaggeration or not, it only added to everyone's fears.

Owned by the City of New Orleans, the Louis Armstrong International Airport is located in Jefferson Parish, with part of the runway extending into St. Charles Parish. When airlines deemed it unsafe to fly, all incoming flights were canceled and aircraft were evacuated north. The cancellations resulted in about 300 people being stranded at the airport. Most of these stranded people happened to be first responders in the medical field who had been attending the National Association of Emergency Medical Technicians Conference held at the New Orleans Convention Center. The convention had just concluded on the day that Hurricane Katrina's path shifted toward New Orleans.

As the floodwaters began to rise in New Orleans and hospitals were forced to abandon their facilities, ill patients started to arrive at the airport, catching the handful of Jefferson Parish Sheriff's deputies by surprise. Concourse D, which normally serviced Delta and Continental Airlines, was transformed into a makeshift triage center. With no pre-planning, no power, no supplies, inadequate staffing, and a non-functional sewage system, the airport would prove to be a less-than-acceptable location. Nonetheless, the critically ill continued to arrive. One benefit that hadn't been seen when the airport was selected as the triage center became obvious, and certainly saved lives: the stranded paramedics provided critical assistance for the overwhelmed medical staff trying to stabilize ill patients in some of the worst conditions imaginable.

With such a large area devastated, shutting down the many highways that allowed access into the flooded and restricted regions was difficult. This placed even more demands on struggling agencies. But manpower shortages didn't just affect the storm-ravaged communities. Agencies in communities outside the destruction were dealing with overnight population explosions, and all the demands that placed on their unprepared communities. Troopers with the Louisiana State Police responded to the area from all across Louisiana and decreased some of the burden on local law enforcement agencies. The entire region was locked down. Only emergency and recovery personnel were allowed in. Many who stayed were desperately trying to leave.

In the St. Charles Emergency Operations Center, I sat in on a teleconference with state officials. Senators David Vitter and Mary Landrieu explained how they had toured the area by helicopter and reported their observations from the aerial survey. They said that all of St. Bernard Parish was flooded. Most of Plaquemines Parish was not only flooded, but also washed away. The Interstate 10 twin span bridges over Lake Pontchartrain, which connect New Orleans and Slidell, had been substantially damaged, with extensive sections washed away. Parts of St. Tammany Parish and Jefferson Parish were devastated, as was the entire Gulf Coast of Mississippi.

In New Orleans, officials reported that additional attempts to block the breaches in the levees had also failed, and that larger sandbags were on their way. Once filled, these bags would weigh several tons each and would hopefully be too large to wash away when dropped by helicopter into the breach. Meanwhile, floodwater continued to flow into the city. There was an apparent need for evacuation at the Superdome and Convention Center. Each parish gave a report and pleaded for help to state officials for both manpower and supplies. I walked away from this meeting with a feeling that there was a tremendous disconnect at the state level. There was so much need for assistance in each parish, but I didn't get the feeling that there was much of a plan at the state level to deal with these needs.

Through their television sets, the entire world was watching images of people trapped on rooftops and hearing horrific reports from inside the Superdome. All attention at the state and federal level was now focused on these needs. And so it should have been, for the need was great. Officers with the Louisiana Wildlife and Fisheries, with boats in tow, arrived in New Orleans in large numbers. They immediately joined in on the search and rescue operations. However, the need was just as demanding in St. Bernard, Plaquemines, St. Tammany, and in Jefferson Parishes. With an overwhelmed state response, each parish was forced to fend for itself.

National Guard Troops that were promised to arrive in St. Charles Parish later that day failed to show. Apparently they had been diverted to other operations. Two National Guardsmen were assigned to the St. Charles Emergency Operations Center as liaison officers between the National Guard and St. Charles Parish, but for the most part, they would be alone for days.

Reports of looting intensified and played out on television screens across the world. With most local television station transmitters underwater for those in the impacted region, only those residents with satellite dishes and generators were able to see these images. The word spread like wildfire. Reports and images of the Oakwood Shopping Mall being set ablaze by looters only added to the fears.

At the Jefferson Parish Sheriff's Office Detective Bureau, detectives working the night shift had set up cots in their offices while the day shift went out on patrol. They were awakened by detectives knocking on doors and repeating a rumor that the gang of thugs who had set the Oakwood Shopping Mall ablaze were headed to the Detective Bureau to take it over. With that rumor, the detectives boarded up the front door of the building and posted armed detectives on the roof and the building perimeter.

As water began to rise in the lower-lying areas of New Orleans at an increasingly alarming rate, many rumors started to reach the Riverfront area of the city. Reports that floodwaters were expected to overrun even the highest parts of the city gave many a reason for concern, and a desire to move to even higher ground. One fire station abandoned its high and dry station house and encouraged the police officers at the relocated sixth district, who had found refuge at a Wal-Mart, to follow them as they moved to the elevated portions of Interstate 10 to protect their firefighters and equipment.

While officers with the New Orleans Harbor Police Department were beginning to pluck survivors off the rooftops of their flooded homes in the Lower Ninth Ward and bring them to higher ground, Cynthia Swain, the Director of Port Safety and Security made the decision to dismiss Harbor employees, including police officers, so they could evacuate for their own safety. This decision did not sit well with Harbor Police Chief Robert Hecker. Defying a direct order, Chief Hecker told his officers what his boss had ordered and gave each of them permission to make their own decisions as he explained his intention to remain on the job, rescuing victims and restoring order to their city. He stayed on the job, as did almost all of his officers.

One incident that wasn't exaggerated was of New Orleans Police Officer Kevin Thomas being shot in the head after confronting looters in Gretna, Louisiana. Officer Thomas and another officer confronted several looters who were stealing merchandise from a Chevron station. One of the officers went inside the store while Thomas remained outside and challenged a man he saw looting the store. When he did, another looter came from behind and shot the officer in the head. Thomas was rushed to West Jefferson Medical Center, where he underwent surgery. The good news was that Thomas was expected to survive. Jefferson Parish deputies arrested four people on the scene. Of those arrested, one was wounded in the arm after exchanging gunfire with another officer.

The rumors, given credibility by media reports of rapes and murders and lawlessness in New Orleans, and the many structural fires reportedly set by looters, caused some jurisdictions to close their borders to anyone trying to leave New Orleans on foot. This was a decision that would later be widely criticized as racially motivated.

With hotel space overburdened in the Baton Rouge area, first responders needed a place for themselves and their families to stay. The Baton Rouge Fraternal Order of Police responded. They turned their 10,000 square feet Lodge Hall on Greenwell Springs Road into a temporary shelter for law enforcement families. All first responders and their families were welcomed with opened arms.

Chest Deep and Rising:

The Baton Rouge Lodge tapped every available resource and provided overnight accommodations and support for over three weeks. These evacuees were police, sheriff deputies, and Emergency Medical Technicians from various jurisdictions in southeast Louisiana. With the help of volunteers from Dream Day Foundation and local church groups, guests at their shelter were fed three meals a day, and transportation was provided for families after some of the officers returned to their duties. Each had an incredible story to tell about their fight for survival. Trained peer counselors were brought in to assist anyone who requested their services; there were plenty who took advantage. The community responded locally and nationally: the Baton Rouge Lodge received truckloads of clothing, food, personal hygiene items and countless other needed goods. These items were available each day and, along with purchased supplies, were transported to first responders in the disaster area.

At an industry meeting in the St. Charles Emergency Operation Center, each plant representative reported on the status of their facility and explained their needs. With two gasoline-producing plants in St. Charles Parish, which make up a significant portion of the nation's gasoline supply, emphasis was placed on helping the plants become operational. For the most part, the plants were in fairly good shape. The movement of supplies in and out of the plants became their immediate concern.

After the meeting, Sheriff Champagne asked me to take Keith Casey, the plant manager of Motiva Enterprises' Norco refinery, to Metairie to get some items from his home. Borrowing Sergeant Mickey Bergeron's police vehicle, a large Ford King Cab pick-up with high clearance, we headed to Metairie and were amazed at the destruction caused by wind damage. Previous reports we had received of the Jefferson Levees breaching were false, but there was extensive flooding throughout Jefferson Parish from rainfall and backflow seeping through non operational drainage pumps. When we approached the Old Metairie area, it was apparent that floodwaters had devastated it. As we neared his home, I found myself once again driving in an area where I was taking on water inside the truck's cab, only this time, going further was not an option. I carefully backed out and tried a different approach. That too failed! Casey was determined to see his home and retrieve some of his wife's personal effects, especially since it was her birthday. He jumped out of the truck into the water and walked to his home in waist-deep water.

Sitting in the truck with water around my ankles, I patiently waited for his return. My cell phone rang, catching me off guard, since my phone hadn't worked in over 28 hours. It was National Fraternal Order of Police President Chuck Canterbury in Myrtle Beach, South Carolina. We were both surprised to make contact. Apparently my Nextel phone hit a functional tower at the same time he was calling. I gave him an overview, and he shared with me the national news coverage. I mentioned the challenges we were experiencing as a result of manpower shortages, and he mentioned that the US Capitol Police might be available to respond. He also mentioned that the Washington, DC, Fraternal Order of Police had offered the use of their mobile kitchen.

Expressing our appreciation, I asked that he make arrangements for both. It was good to talk to him. I knew many of my friends nationwide were concerned and I felt better knowing Chuck would convey to them that I had made out okay. Since I had a cell phone signal, I then called my wife, Gail. I was relieved to learn my family had made out fine;

however, the power was out and the heat was getting the best of them in a house that had poor air circulation. Gail decided she was coming home that evening.

Minutes later, Casey waded back towards the truck with two carrying cases in tow. He threw the cases into the bed of the truck and climbed into the cab. He said that there was about three feet of water in his new home and that pretty much everything was ruined. As we headed back to St. Charles Parish, I admired his very positive and upbeat attitude. Sitting in the truck, soaking wet from having walked to his flooded home, Casey spoke more of his concern for his employees' homes and his need to establish temporary housing for them than he did of his own personal crisis.

I dropped him off at the refinery and drove by the hospital to check on my guys, and then went back to the St. Charles Emergency Operations Center for updates. About ready to call it a night, on the way home, I rolled backup on a Suspicious Persons call in the Ormond Subdivision area. Reports of looting had put people on edge and created a frenzy I had never before experienced. Normally levelheaded people, confused and fearful, were seeing things that didn't exist. Signs stating that looters would be shot had popped up on many corners. Seeing people sitting in their front yards on lawn chairs with shotguns lying across their laps, watching over their and their neighbor's property, had become commonplace.

Late in the day, the news carried Department of Homeland Security Secretary Michael Chertoff's declaration that Hurricane Katrina had been designated an "Incident of National Significance," triggering for the first time a coordinated national security response.

In the coming days, the magnitude of just how significant an event this would prove to be also showed America just

---

how unprepared she really was to deal with such a major event.

Exhausted, I returned home at around 11:00 P.M. With Hurricane Katrina now declared an event of national significance, I was hopeful that the next day, the "Calvary" would come and help augment our resources. Gail and the girls were home. We shared our experiences and stories about the storm and all slept in the living room, where the small air conditioning window unit had cooled the room. You don't realize how much you depend on air conditioning until you lose it for a few days. Man, was that great!

Day Six
Wednesday, August 31, 2005

It Just Kept Getting Worse

Wednesday, August 31st would be one of the most demanding days experienced thus far. In more intense heat, with very little breeze to move the stale air, my day started very early with a quick trip to Jackie Bee's to fuel my police car. Those who had stayed quickly learned that getting supplies to sustain themselves would be a bit challenging. In a time when ATM and debit cards had become a way of life, the collapse of electronic commerce meant that cash was the only means of acquiring goods. The need for cash caught many off guard, including myself. The manager at Jackie Bee's was kind enough to allow me to open a personal account for fuel to keep my home generator running.

I returned home with 20 gallons of extremely expensive fuel. Fuel prices across the United States had skyrocketed, a casualty of Hurricane Katrina's impact on oil production and the shutdown of eight refineries in the region. I stopped to talk to another neighbor who had returned home late the night before. He looked exhausted. Sleeping in intense heat with no breeze is brutal, and the effects on him and his wife were apparent. I offered to hook up an extension cord to my generator to power a fan. They wasted no time plugging in.

Arriving for the 9:00 A.M. meeting at the St. Charles Parish Emergency Operations Center, Sheriff Champagne pulled me aside and asked what I planned to do that day. He went on to say that he had been running for four days non-stop with very little sleep, and was exhausted. I offered to make the rounds with the Sheriff that day.

He relayed a series of conversations and text messages he had received that ended up having a big impact on the day's activities. In the early morning hours he had received a call from Earl Tastet, a St. Charles Parish Justice of the Peace, who asked if the Sheriff would call a Luling resident who had evacuated to the Dallas area. The man, David Riddick, needed assistance in rescuing his wife from the Ernest Morial Convention Center in New Orleans. Using a satellite phone, Sheriff Champagne called Mr. Riddick, who explained that he'd spoken to his wife, Renee, who, along with about 50 or so other nurses and staff, had been transported from the flooded Memorial Hospital to the Convention Center, where they were to catch a bus—a bus that never arrived. He was maintaining contact with her through text messages on their cell phones, which seemed to be far more reliable than getting through by voice call.

According to Mr. Riddick, the group had found themselves in a part of the Convention Center where thugs were threatening and robbing others. Every time they tried to move away from the thugs, they were harassed and threatened. The thugs had gained control over the group through intimidation. The hospital group refused to break up, and many were too afraid to leave out of fear of retaliation. Mr. Riddick asked Sheriff Champagne to rescue his wife from the Convention

Chest Deep and Rising:

Center. This was a request that sounded reasonable, but one that was not practical in the environment of that day, given that there were three jurisdictional boundaries between St. Charles Parish and the Convention Center. There was also no communication with the other extremely overwhelmed agencies. With communications almost nonexistent, coordinating such an action wasn't possible. Sheriff Champagne encouraged Mr. Riddick to convince his wife to walk across the Crescent City Connection, a high-rise bridge leading out of the City of New Orleans. Once across the bridge, the Sheriff would provide transportation to safety.

On that Wednesday, we all began to realize that life was different post-Katrina. What a difference a few miles make! At the St. Charles Parish Emergency Operations Center 9:00 A.M. briefing, extensive plans were taking shape as we quickly moved into recovery mode. Yet, just a few miles away, the scene was much more intense. People were still being rescued from their rooftops, an estimated 40,000 people were trapped inside the Louisiana Superdome, another 15,000 at the Convention Center, and reports of looting and vandalism were rampant. All state and federal resources had been quickly directed to solving the problems with the most publicity. Promises of National Guard support kept being pulled and diverted elsewhere. Although frustrated, we certainly understood that the demands were greater elsewhere. I mentioned to the Sheriff my conversation with Chuck Canterbury and the availability of Capitol Police being deployed, and he was very pleased. The growing demands were quickly exceeding our staffing levels. This was something that would surely get worse as time went on.

In addition to the growing problems in the city, St. Charles Parish witnessed unfolding events. Food, water, and ice started to arrive in an unexpectedly high volume. Fearful of the televised lawlessness, delivery drivers were looking for a better way to deliver to New Orleans. St. Charles Parish became their desired location because it was the closest to the flooded area. Under the supervision of Jim Polk, a co-ordinator in the St. Charles Emergency Operation Center, a food, ice, and water distribution network was developed at the Westbank Bridge Park, at the base of the Interstate Bridge. Traveling from all across the impacted region, traffic snaked through the large recreation park for days. The line spilled onto the shoulder of the highway, then down a long, remote street. In all, a thousand cars a day could wait in line and not create any substantial traffic problems. Recipients never exited their vehicles; they drove through and were handed items through the windows, or community volunteers and trustees from the St. Charles Parish Correctional Center placed items in their trunks. Once word got out about the site, thousands of citizens flocked to it daily. It served as a perfect example of "thinking outside the box" and making good things happen. But it also placed tremendous demands on our limited and fatigued personnel.

As supplies were delivered, Hurricane Katrina acquainted us with many new experiences and gave us new words for our everyday vocabulary. One such example is something I never really took a liking to: the introduction of MREs (Meals Ready to Eat). Modern battlefield requirements demand ration support systems that adequately provide for the nutritional needs of the individual soldier in extremely intense and highly mobile combat situations. The standard military ration for an individual is the MRE. The MRE maintains high quality for up to three years. This makes it the perfect way to feed people in times of disaster. They served their purpose and even offered some entertainment. Others and myself may not have liked the lack of taste, but it did offer an alternative to starving or eating stockpiles of Spam and other canned delicacies.

Banks, stores, and industrial facilities began requesting that deputies be assigned to their locations; we simply didn't have enough manpower. I again reminded the Sheriff of the availability of Capitol Police. After successfully getting in touch with Canterbury, the official request for Capitol Police was made.

A seventy-year-old African American lady was found walking west on the Mississippi River Levee. She had fled Gretna, LA, on foot in the middle of the night and had walked all night to reach the St. Charles Parish line, a distance of 20 miles. She was picked up and given food and water before transportation was arranged for her to Baton Rouge. Her determination and pleasant attitude were an inspiration. She wasn't the only one walking west to escape New Orleans. Other jurisdictions, however, were handling this migration differently, and many were criticized for their perceived lack of compassion.

In St. Charles Parish, the remedy was to set up staging areas at the St. Charles/Jefferson Parish line, where pedestrians were put on a bus and transported to Eual J. Landry Middle School, located next to the St. Charles Parish Courthouse. There, evacuees were fed, given an opportunity to clean up, rest, and were transported on to a permanent shelter in Baton Rouge, where they would be routed to one of the many shelters opening across Louisiana. This approach had a couple of benefits. First and foremost, it helped people who desperately needed help. It also eliminated pedestrians walking through neighborhoods and encountering edgy residents sitting on lawn chairs with guns in hand. This would have placed even more manpower demands on the department.

At a meeting with industrial representatives, additional problems arose. Several plants had the ability to transport gasoline to areas in desperate need, but road closures and severe traffic prevented their ability to make adequate deliveries. Escorts and authorizing access to closed roadways offered some relief, but this service continued to stretch our already exhausted resources.

Leaving the Courthouse for a trip to Jackie Bee's to fuel up, Sheriff Champagne wanted to pass by his home to drop something off. It was there that I realized what all the paranoia was about. For the first time, watching his Direct TV, I saw the live images of lawlessness, looting, homes and a shopping mall set ablaze, with no means of extinguishing the fire. I also saw horrific conditions at the Superdome and Convention Center. Reports of murder and rape were being reported endlessly… no wonder everyone was on edge. If this was what the entire world was seeing, it offered an explanation as to why so many cops were reportedly walking off the job. Their families, through rare cell phone conversations, were no doubt demanding it.

While Sheriff Champagne was at his home, he received additional text messages from Mr. Riddick, who continued to plead for help for his wife and co-workers. He relayed that his wife and the other medical staff had refused to attempt the walk out of New Orleans. They feared that some in the group would not be physically able to walk the distance and by that time, rumors were prevalent that African-Americans were being shot at as they attempted to cross the bridge. Because several in the group were African-American, they had voted to stay together, even if it meant staying in New Orleans. The feeling of helplessness caused Sheriff Champagne to become very emotional. We talked about trying a rescue, but at the same time, he didn't want to put even more lives in jeopardy in a rescue operation outside his jurisdiction.

Cellular service started working sporadically. The best results were calls outside the 504 area code. It was certainly a lesson in humility. It would take 20 or so attempts before getting through, and that usually ended with a dropped call after a minute or so. I was able to get through on my cell phone to Johnny Frederic and Tommy Tizzard, who had all weathered the storm well. They, along with their wives and volunteers, were manning the Fraternal Order of Police office phones in Baton Rouge. They were overwhelmed with offers from people across the country wishing to volunteer, send supplies, get messages to law enforcement members in affected areas, pledges for financial assistance; the list went on and on.

Both Tizzard and Frederic were on their way to the Baton Rouge Airport to greet a helicopter en route from the Louisiana Superdome. They were to pick up Jefferson Parish Sheriff's Deputy Kevin Balser, Willie Patin's son-in-law, and bring him to the elevated portion of Interstate 10, alongside the Louisiana Superdome. There, he would retrieve his police car and report back to duty in Jefferson Parish. Willie Patin, his wife, Ivonne, their pregnant daughter, Kim, and a couple of coworkers had ridden out Hurricane Katrina in what they had thought would be the plush corporate office of his employer on Poydras Street, across from the Louisiana Superdome.

On duty in Jefferson Parish during the storm, Deputy Balser was granted permission to check on his pregnant wife, just over the parish line in New Orleans. Once there, he was trapped. As the floodwaters rose, they evacuated vertically into the higher floors of the building and watched the chaos at the Superdome unfold before their eyes. Battling intense heat in a building with fixed windows, they were eventually able to make telephone contact with representatives of Patin's company, who gave him permission to abandon the building. His employer hired a Sikorsky Executive Series Helicopter, the only helicopter available for hire at the time. After calling in major political favors and convincing the helicopter's owner that the National Guard had the landing area secure, the pilot was granted permission to land at the Superdome helipad, by then designated a military landing zone. They were to board the helicopter and be taken to safety. There was only one very big problem: they had to wade through the floodwaters to the Superdome, where thousands were also trying to evacuate.

Patin and his crew had two very real concerns. First, how would he get his pregnant daughter to the Superdome without having her walk through contaminated floodwaters, which by then had developed a foamy sheen on the surface, composed of raw sewage, motor oil and gasoline from submerged vehicles, and you could only imagine what else. Just as troubling, having for two days watched in disgust as the chaos developed, even if they did make it safely to the helipad, what if they were denied access to their helicopter and forced into the chaos?

Knowing time was short, Patin wasted no time in placing his daughter on an inflatable mattress and floating her across the floodwaters, as the others in the group waded through chest deep. Once they reached the Superdome, afraid to discard the air mattress in case they needed to retreat to the office building, Patin carried the air mattress right up until the time he boarded the helicopter. Finally, they were airborne without any problems, and in the comfort only the highest-level executives are accustomed to. They were off to the Baton Rouge Airport. Ironically, their flight path took them over their flooded home in Metairie.

Back in St. Charles Parish, moving trucks, dump body trucks, delivery vans, and the like all passed through the parish, traveling west on US Hwy 90. Many were loaded with people standing shoulder to shoulder. Seemingly any vehicle that was operational was used, some with 30 or 40 people onboard. The Louisiana State Police stopped one such vehicle, a Heineken beer delivery truck. Inside the truck cab and storage bins were 19 people, several new televisions, other high-end electronics, and a bag full of money. Watching delivery trucks loaded with people, it was easier to assume they had permission to use the trucks; deputies just kept the traffic flowing out of the flooded city. But now, because of the traffic stop by Louisiana State Police, and with the occupants' claim that they had found the truck with the keys in it, deputies were faced with a dilemma. Were these people criminals, or citizens trying to flee a horrible situation? All of the suspected looted items and the occupants were taken to the St. Charles Parish Correctional Center.

Something to Offer Hope

After responding to two more suspicious persons calls, we headed back to the Courthouse for a 2:00 P.M. meeting at the St. Charles Emergency Operation Center. After the meeting, St. Charles Parish Councilman Barry Minnich approached the Sheriff and myself and asked for help. He had spoken to his son-in-law, a nurse at Memorial Hospital, who advised that he was abandoning the hospital due to flooding. Jarred Fuslier intended to wade through the water to the Mississippi River Levee and walk to St. Charles Parish.

They had not heard from him for hours, and asked

if someone could enter the city to look for him. Lieutenant Wayne Lee, a supervisor in the Sheriff's Office's Information Technology Division, with over 20 years' law enforcement experience, and myself volunteered. Along with Councilman Minnich, the three of us drove into New Orleans on top of the east bank Mississippi Levee, to bypass floodwaters as we dodged downed power lines, trees, and debris in hopes we would find Jarred walking along the levee. A Jefferson Levee Board Police Officer stopped us and asked what we were doing. I explained, and he gave us directions around impassable areas. He also suggested we rethink our plans. We knew our efforts were a "long shot," but proceeded.

Driving through New Orleans was surreal. People were pushing overloaded shopping carts down streets filled with looted goods, doors had been kicked in, windows were shattered, and every retail business we passed appeared to have been burglarized. At the entrance of one drug store, a parked forklift held the burglar bars raised, allowing access for looters. Reports on the radio explained how rescue helicopters had started taking gunfire from the crowds below. The city was out of control.

Although we were in an unmarked Durango, a few people recognized my uniform and cursed us. We traveled along the dry portion of the Garden District and Uptown areas in our search. Our travels brought us very close to the Convention Center. On famed St. Charles Avenue, where stately mansions line the oak-covered boulevard, thugs were seen sitting on the second floor gallery of a mansion, taking in the good life as they watched the occasional police vehicle zoom by. Society had fallen apart; there were no laws, no right or wrong, no order. People were doing as they wished, with absolutely no fear of consequences.

After a couple of hours of searching unsuccessfully, even Councilman Minnich knew we were running out of luck. We decided we would make one last pass by Napoleon and St. Charles Avenues, where New Orleans Police had set up a staging area to bus people out of the city. We had already made one unsuccessful pass there. As we made the block, getting ready to travel back to St. Charles Parish, Councilman Minnich jumped out of the rolling truck, yelling "Jarred, Jarred..." as the two embraced. Jarred was fine. He and five others had stopped to help at the staging area. I quickly directed them all into the Durango, and away all nine of us, and their two dogs, went, cramped in the vehicle, headed back to St. Charles Parish. They talked nonstop of their experiences. I was able to make contact with Sheriff Champagne, using Nextel Direct Connect, and advised him we had six rescued and were heading home. He tried to answer, but you could hear cheers and excitement in the background from others in the St. Charles Emergency Operations Center as they drowned out his words. It was good news at a time when we all needed it.

We drove to the Luling Firehouse, where we were met by scores of family members and friends who were excited to see their loved ones returned safe. Sheriff Champagne met us there and was just as excited as the family members. After days of endless bad news, this was a boost for everyone. But the trip did leave me numb. Hearing rumors of the lawlessness was one thing; actually seeing a city out of control was another. The experience fostered a wide range of emotions, from compassion to anger. It was a sickening feeling.

Reports of the deteriorating conditions in New Orleans were upsetting. By Wednesday evening, Louisiana Governor Blanco had issued orders for emergency occupation of hotel and motel rooms and authorized the commandeering and use of buses for evacuation and relief efforts. An exodus from the Superdome began, with the first buses leaving for Houston's Astrodome, 350 miles away.

Mayor Nagin ordered the New Orleans Police Department to leave their search-and-rescue mission and return to the streets of New Orleans, to stop looting that had turned increasingly hostile. "They are starting to get closer to heavily populated areas—hotels, hospitals—and we're going to stop it right now," Nagin commented to news reporters, as he pleaded for more federal help. With parts of Interstate 10 submerged, each bus, as with every vehicle trying to flee New Orleans, was forced to travel the congested four-lane US Hwy 90 through St. Charles Parish.

Having cut his vacation short at his ranch in Crawford, Texas, President George Bush headed back to the White House. Air Force One was seen flying low over the region, allowing the President to survey the damage over the Gulf South Region. Shortly after 5:00 P.M., he held a press conference in the Rose Garden of the White House, where he detailed his strategy for short-term recovery efforts. This included the deployment of 30,000 National Guardsman, although it would take days before any arrived. This gave way to hope that help would soon be on its way.

New Orleans Convention Center

During the time we were searching in New Orleans, Sheriff Champagne received several more text messages and calls from Mr. Riddick. He advised that his wife's text messages were getting desperate and explained her belief that they would not survive the night. Lieutenant Lee and I told the

Sheriff that we had been able to drive close to the Convention Center and felt very confident that we could get a bus there to remove the nurses. We suggested taking a ride there in an unmarked car to assess the situation. Sheriff Champagne agreed.

In an unmarked police car, Captain Jonathan Walsdorf, Lieutenant Wayne Lee and Staff Sgt. Dan Beier of the Louisiana National Guard traveled to the Convention Center with specific tasks: assess the environment at the Convention Center, attempt to locate a New Orleans Police Officer or National Guardsman assigned to that area in hopes of coordinating the rescue, scout out the best location to park the bus into which to load the nurses and, most important, see how difficult it would be to identify the group of nurses in such a chaotic environment.

Arriving at the Convention Center, the men were unable to locate police or National Guardsmen. If they were there, certainly the masses of people would make finding them impossible. They observed thousands of people standing on the streets and sidewalks. Several burned and vandalized vehicles were parked along the roadway, some still smoldering. A disabled New Orleans Police Department police car near the Convention Center was severely damaged. The windows were busted out, and the tires removed; people sat on the police car as if it were their own personal property.

As they drove slowly down Convention Center Boulevard, obscenities of every nature were shouted, with some in the crowd aggressively trying to stop their vehicle. Near the intersection of Henderson Street, a group of mostly women wearing hospital scrubs was observed on the opposite side of the street from the Center.

Pulling up beside them, Captain Walsdorf asked if they were okay. They stared in silence, afraid to answer. One woman finally spoke up, "No, we're not okay! We are going to be dead by morning!" The woman quickly explained that they were evacuees from Memorial Hospital and had been forced out by the floodwaters. She went on to explain how the crowd was "about half good, honest, poor people" who had helped them defend themselves from the other half, the "thugs." She leaned into the police car and mentioned that her husband had been talking with a sheriff who was supposed to send someone to rescue them. After the men explained who they were, the group was excited. Captain Walsdorf promised they would return within two hours with a vehicle large enough to evacuate everyone in the group.

Through a Nextel call from Captain Walsdorf, he advised the Sheriff that they had indeed located the group. We talked briefly about the location and a preliminary plan and started the ball rolling as they drove back with more detailed information about the location. After convincing Sheriff Champagne that we could accomplish this mission, he gave us permission to move forward. I can only imagine the anxiety he experienced during the hours that followed. If we were successful, he would be a hero for taking such unusual steps to rescue helpless people in a time of desperate need. If one single thing went wrong—and the odds of that were certainly more likely—that, too, would reflect upon him in ways that, I am sure, ran endlessly through his mind. The courage needed for his decision was far more demanding than the actions of those carrying out the rescue mission.

Quickly devising a plan, a team of 14, headed by Chief Cardella, was assembled. A quick response was not only necessary, but it was actually working in our favor at that point. The team was in an excellent position to remove the group with little complications; a delay could decrease our effectiveness.

The 14 members of the team participating in the operation were Chief Deputy Joseph Cardella, Captain Jonathan Walsdorf, Lieutenant Rodney Madere, Sergeants Roscoe Brewer and Wayne Joseph, Deputies Ryan Ordner, David Ehrmann, and Deputy Douglas Carter, Detective Steve Gonzales, Lieutenant Wayne Lee, and myself with the St. Charles Sheriff's Office, Gary Martin, St. Charles Parish School System's Transportation Director, and Staff Sgt. Rob L'Huillier and Staff Sgt. Dan Beier 1/244th CAB, Alpha Co., LA Army National Guard, Lakefront Airport.

When Walsdorf, Lee, and Beier returned to the St. Charles Emergency Operation Center, they explained their findings. Walsdorf explained that for the rescue mission to be successful, it would have to be both swift and dynamic. Walsdorf expressed his concern that if the crowd became aware of the operation, they would most certainly swarm the group and attempt to commandeer the bus. The situation could potentially escalate and become desperate.

From bus driver to diversion, from providing cover to addressing medical needs, each deputy had his own assignments. We walked though the plan in detail. Then we strapped on ballistic vests and riot gear, armed ourselves with enough firepower to take over a small country, loaded onto a yellow school bus and two unmarked police vehicles, and headed to the Convention Center. Riding on the bus, we continued to discuss our different roles. The objective was to load everyone on the bus in no more than two minutes and drive up the ramp, before the thugs congregating at that section of the Convention Center realized what was taking place.

The bus pulled up to its assigned position at the entrance ramp to the Crescent City Connection Mississippi Bridge at Tchoptoulas and Henderson Streets, where we piled out and set up a secure perimeter. There was very little moonlight, and just the silhouettes of the high-rise office buildings, hotels and the Convention Center could be seen. Only the spotlights of the National Guard Helicopters that crisscrossed the sky pierced the darkness. That image alone made the hair on the back of my neck stand on end. The darkness helped mask the yellow school bus parked less than a block away from the Convention Center, across a parking lot with several trailers. I could make out the outline of a large mass of people, but I am sure the trailers obscured their view. With no way to communicate with first responders and National Guardsmen in the area, I wondered to myself how the National Guard helicopter crews would respond if they saw 14 people dressed in black, carrying rifles.

Captain Walsdorf approached the group and told them to walk slowly to the street corner, where a bus was waiting. Some were too anxious to do as instructed, and broke out in a full run towards the corner, where several others and I were waiting. This caught the attention of some of the thugs, who started to move towards the group of nurses.

As the nurses approached the bus, I received their bags and threw them onto the curb to make room for the reported 50 nurses and eight members of the team on a single bus. I directed them to the door, where Gary Martin lifted them onto the bus. As I threw the bags, I could tell some were distraught about the loss of their possessions, but I was more concerned with immediately getting the people on the bus and getting back to St. Charles Parish before we found ourselves being confronted by the band of thugs.

An elderly African-American gentleman in the group stood and said to Walsdorf, "I have to get my wife. She has bad knees and can't walk too good... She's across the street, right over there," as the man gestured toward the Convention Center. The man broke from the group, crossed the street, and went into the crowd. Captain Walsdorf followed him onto the median and awaited his return as the people lining the street began to stir and become aware of the situation. The man exclaimed to his wife in the midst of the evacuees, "Let's go, we're getting out of here." This immediately resulted in commotion from other evacuees in the area. Flashlights snapped on to spotlight Captain Walsdorf. Angry and threatening words soon followed from the crowd.

Some of the crowd walked menacingly toward Captain Walsdorf, taunting him with profanity and other inciting comments. The crowd grew closer, and the verbal threats escalated. Walsdorf later reflected that they moved like "zombies" as they approached him. They were desperate to escape, and it was obvious they would do absolutely anything to make that happen.

Lieutenant Madere returned with his police vehicle as the elderly man emerged from the crowd with his wife. The woman, who had great difficulty walking, was quickly placed in the front seat of the unmarked police vehicle. The officers made sure that all were safely accounted for. Before the thugs could decide how to react, the bus departed, loaded with twenty-eight people. Men, women, and children, white, African-American, two Australian tourists, had all been rescued. The whole operation took no more than a couple of minutes, and we were on the road, getting further away from the hell at the Convention Center with every passing second. Initial reports were that some of the group might need medical attention. We had planned to bring them to West Jefferson Hospital, the closest operational hospital in the area. After a quick assessment of everyone's condition, we decided instead to take the group to St. Charles Parish Hospital. We advised Dispatch to notify the hospital of our anticipated arrival.

On the bus ride back, we repeatedly conducted a head-count to ensure the presence of all team members. There was panic from a mother who couldn't find her child. It concerned us enough to stop the bus and unmarked police cars on the side of the Westbank Expressway. Out of breath as she rushed toward the bus, the mother had instinctively handed her infant child to one of the deputies through a car window. Radio interference made it difficult to clearly understand that everyone was accounted for. While stopped alongside the road, we confirmed the child was in an accompanying police car, and I was relieved. The possibility of returning to the Convention Center to search for the child and doing so without the advantage of surprise was not a pleasant thought, but one for a moment we had had to contemplate.

Once back on the road, I realized the group was shocked and confused. They sat quietly, some crying, others hugging each other. They had little idea of what had just happened. All they knew was that 14 men, dressed in riot gear and brandishing automatic weapons, had rushed them onto a bus that was now traveling to an unknown location. As we passed out bottled water, I explained to everyone that they had been rescued by the St. Charles Parish Sheriff's Office, and we were on our way back to civilization. With that single explanation, the expressions on their faces changed from pure fear to total elation, as if a switch had been flipped. They all began to cheer. Tears of fear turned to tears of joy. They smiled as they clapped. Minutes earlier, they had seemed passive; now they talked about their ordeal. It was as if they had to compete with each other to express themselves. Chief Cardella went to the rear seat of the bus and sat next to one of the nurses, to appear less threatening, while other members of the team took seats in different parts of the bus and engaged the nurses in conversation.

One by one, they chimed in with descriptions of total lawlessness. Their stories were amazing. Every one of them felt they would not have survived much longer. One pointed out that the thugs were clearly in charge. All had heard gunfire often, and frequently were threatened at gunpoint. The only appearance of authority was a young man wearing a security guard uniform and driving around on a motorized cart as he barked out orders. He looked like he was in charge, so for the most part, he was. Everyone seemed to follow his instructions. However, as time progressed, his orders made no sense and with that, he began losing his authority status. Another advised that the National Guard was there, but they were so far away from the people, they seemed more focused on containing the crowd than offering any assistance or protection. Yet another insisted the only reason they were alive was because of the African-American members of their group who spoke out against the thugs who singled out members of the group because of their race.

The mood changed as I filled the group in on the bigger picture of what was going on in the Gulf South Region, and advised them that Hurricane Katrina would be recognized as the worst natural disaster in American history. Unfortunately, I also relayed some of the information I had obtained from government and media sources, information that was later proven to be exaggerated or false. Nonetheless, perception is reality, and the perception was that there had been a total meltdown, with tens of thousands dead.

I spoke to one lady who was clearly upset and asked her if she was okay. She explained that the bags we had left on the curbside contained jewelry given to her by her mother. I apologized profusely and went to the back of the bus and advised Chief Cardella I wanted to go back to the Convention Center to pick up the bags. He refused the request, stating that he would not test fate only to recover property. I hadn't given any thought to what might be in the bags. It had been part of our pre-planning; we thought we would have an overloaded bus with over 50 nurses and eight deputies. Having an opportunity to do this over again, I would have gone back to retrieve the bags and begged for the Chief's forgiveness upon my return. This would prove to be one of my biggest regrets of the entire Hurricane Katrina ordeal.

Arriving at St. Charles Parish Hospital, we saw that a large group of people had gathered outside the emergency room door, awaiting our arrival. As the passengers exited the bus, the crowd cheered and cameras flashed. Everyone was excited and the Sheriff relieved. We had returned home safely without incident. He would later claim these were perhaps the longest two hours in his life.

Medical staff at the hospital gave each survivor a checkup. The rescued groups showered for the first time in days and were brought into the cafeteria, where they received their first hot meal since Hurricane Katrina. Some used satellite phones to call family and let them know they were fine. Also rescued were several pets: a few dogs, a cat, and a gerbil. Jena Troxler, a local veterinarian and wife of St. Charles Emergency Operations Center Director Tab Troxler, took the pets home with her.

Shopping for a second opinion, I asked Sheriff Champagne for permission to return to the Convention Center to recover the bags. He, too, denied my request, for the same reasons. I knew they were both right, but it didn't make me feel any better. I thought of the family heirlooms I cherish and couldn't stop thinking about how I would feel had I lost them.

While all were seated in the hospital cafeteria, visibly emotional, Sheriff Champagne explained the events and challenges of the day that had led up to their rescue. He talked about the text messages and calls he had received from Mr. Riddick, his frustration and feelings of helplessness, and his anxiety in making the decision to send his deputies into a city where he had no authority, no ability to communicate with other agencies, and very little pre-planning. Then, as his eyes teared up, he talked about his elation when he learned the operation had been successful.

Over the next hour or so, the group took turns relaying their experiences during the storm, and describing the hellish environment at the Convention Center. One nurse explained how an elderly woman at the Convention Center had died after suffering a high fever for over 18 hours. Several thugs had taken the body from family members and loaded it onto a motorized cart used by the Convention Center maintenance crew. They had paraded the lifeless body throughout the crowd of evacuees, yelling, "Look, this is what they are doing to us!" The deceased woman's family was obviously distraught; their nightmare only grew worse as the thugs exploited the situation to inflame the crowd.

The two Australians, Fiona Seidel and Katie McLean from Brisbane, were vacationing in the US and had arrived in New Orleans only hours before Hurricane Katrina stuck. They had ridden out the storm at the Monteleon Hotel on Royale Street. They questioned why American Airlines had allowed them to leave Las Vegas for New Orleans and not explained the dangers that awaited them in this evacuated city. They had praise for the hotel, which, they said, spent $20,000 to hire buses to take the hotel guests out of the city. The buses, however, had been commandeered by city officials and rerouted to the Superdome, to be used in the evacuation efforts. When their hotel could not remain open, the two women walked to the Convention Center, where they were told buses would pick them up and take them out of the city. Once at the Convention Center, they befriended the nurses.

One nurse talked about what she referred to as her darkest hours. She, her husband and her son had spent five days in the darkness of Memorial Hospital, watching patients dying before them—only able to offer them warm water to drink and warm breeze from cardboard fans. They tried to offer the patients encouragement and prayed with some who were dying. In all, 45 deaths had occurred at this flooded hospital before, during, and immediately after the storm. She commented that when she thought it could not get any worse, they were evacuated into hell, the Convention Center.

Another spoke of the threats and intimidation they had experienced, and how the heat, misinformation, hopelessness, and lack of food and water had diminished their will to survive. The stories went on and on. Family members started showing up to reunite with their loved ones. With each, the whole emotional process would be relived time and time again. A proud and hardened cop, I tried to fight back my emotions, determined not to allow my coworkers see them. That didn't work, and tears streamed down my face. I wasn't alone, my coworkers, too, were overcome with emotion as well.

Next to the hospital cafeteria was a bulletin board filled with notices and memos. St. Charles Parish Hospital Staff removed all the memos, revealing a yellow backdrop. There, each survivor took turns writing their memories of the Convention Center ordeal and their appreciation for the rescuers and the hospital staff who made them feel at home.

After attending an after-action debriefing meeting, where we routinely review tactical operations and learn from each experience, I drove home feeling helpless and angry in equal portions. We had rescued 28 people from a nightmare, but we had left behind thousands more who were just as desperate. I tried to reason as to how such a thing could continue to get worse and worse. The thoughts sickened me.

Exhausted, I rolled into my home around 3:30 A.M. Wednesday had clearly been the darkest day since Katrina left the Gulf South in ruins. At the height of hopelessness, the rescues of that day gave everyone in St. Charles Parish hope. From this day on, at least in St. Charles Parish, everything seemed to be a little easier. Unfortunately, for many in parishes east of us, the nightmare would continue to rage on for days.

Day Seven
Thursday, September 1, 2005

Becoming Resourceful

I got off to a late start on Thursday, September 1st, missing most of the 9:00 A.M. briefing at the St. Charles Emergency Operation Center. Just as the days before, one of the first orders of business was to get fuel for both my police car and generator. As I arrived at the Courthouse around 9:30 A.M., Sheriff Champagne was outside, trying to make calls on a handheld satellite phone. One by one, he was going down a list of numbers. He had called elated families and advised them that their loved ones had been rescued from the Convention Center. He had called an upset mother in Australia, who was frantically watching international coverage of the storm on her television as she waited near the phone, hoping to hear from her daughter and daughter-in-law, vacationing in New Orleans. The Sheriff's words ended her worry.

The excitement of the previous day's successes was short-lived. The promised National Guard troops were again put off until the next day. This response sounded awfully familiar; the same had been repeated to the evacuees at the Convention Center each day since the storm struck. I was able to contact Chuck Canterbury, who advised that U.S. Capitol Police Chief Terry Gainer was prepared to send 100 Capitol police officers to help, and had received approval from Senate Majority Leader Bill Frist, a surgeon by trade who himself would respond to New Orleans and assist in providing medical assistance to evacuees. However, FEMA was blocking the deployment, calling it a "self-dispatch" since the request had not been approved by that agency. The biggest hold-up was that the request needed to be approved by the Governor's office. This office had already demonstrated its inability to answer our request for additional law enforcement. He assured me that he and Fraternal Order of Police Executive Director Jim Pasco had not given up, and were trying to work through the issue. I could sense his frustration.

With the bureaucratic red tape blocking desperately needed help, our feelings of helplessness gave way to the anger of abandonment, as word quickly spread about comments made by House Majority Leader Dennis Hastert in a Chicago newspaper, suggesting that rebuilding New Orleans didn't "make sense."

Concerned about the growing demands on our manpower needs, I mentioned to Sheriff Champagne that we could easily get much-needed help, but it would go against the grain of FEMA. Since the Sheriff is a constitutionally elected law enforcement officer, he has the right to ask for assistance from other agencies, regardless of FEMA regulations. I relayed the calls of support I had received prior to the storm's arrival. Sheriff Champagne gave permission to send out a call for assistance through the Fraternal Order of Police. The following message went out by email:

Chest Deep and Rising:

Greetings,

We are seeking assistance in St. Charles Parish, just west of New Orleans. We are, for the most part, the only access into Jefferson and Orleans Parishes, which are still affected by floodwater. We have addressed our flooding concerns and are stable, with power being restored. We have established a staging location for services for the region.

We are seeking assistance in traffic checkpoints, and patrol. We have housing and food, but we do not have bedding. We suggest any officer willing to volunteer bring whatever they will need to make themselves comfortable.

Responding officers should have uniforms, side arms, ammunition, and be prepared to be self-sufficient for at least one day. Also, please bring credentials from your agency.

Responding officers are to report to Destrehan High School, following directions off Map Quest. You will need to bypass New Orleans and enter from the west.

Air travel will be difficult; New Orleans International is closed and I do not have means of providing transportation from airports.

Any assistance would be appreciated.

Seemingly within minutes, the calls started flowing in on my cell phone. By the end of the day, we had received commitments from 43 law enforcement agencies from 20 states and some 300 law enforcement officers. In fact, the response was so overwhelming that I recorded a thank you message on my voicemail, explaining that due to the overwhelming response, we had received the manpower assistance needed for now and would send additional requests as needed.

Sheriff Champagne wasn't the only person becoming concerned with the lack of manpower. The Louisiana Sheriff's Task Force had mobilized to assist in water rescues in the City of New Orleans only hours after the storm passed and the levee breaches had occurred. As the crises grew, Ascension Parish Sheriff Jeff Willey, who also serves as President of the Louisiana Sheriff's Association, activated a second phase of the Task Force to assist in the many traffic control points, and to open an evacuation shelter at the Lamar-Dixon Center in Gonzales. With officers responding from all across the state, Sheriff Willey opened a law enforcement shelter at the Lamar-Dixon Center for deputies as well. With each parish in the state dealing with the increase in population and shelters and hotels filled, the demands on every law enforcement agency grew.

As conditions further deteriorated in New Orleans, frustrated with the lack of assistance from state and Federal agencies, the Louisiana Sheriff's Association issued a national call for assistance. Over the days that followed, the law enforcement shelter swelled in size, as just over 1,000 law enforcement officers from 135 agencies responded. With the added manpower, security escorts were assigned to rescue teams in each of the devastated parishes.

Wal-Mart would prove to be a generous partner in supplying first responders with desperately needed supplies. Only days after the storm passed, large Wal-Mart tractor-trailers filled with bottled water and clothing started arriving throughout the New Orleans Metro Area. In Jefferson Parish, Wal-Mart stores that were not flooded and had generator power not only offered supplies, but allowed emergency workers to sleep inside the stores. The quick response of Wal-Mart, in contrast with the sluggish response of state and federal assistance, was explained through comments made by Jefferson Parish Sheriff Harry Lee, who noted that if responding state and federal agencies had acted as quickly as Wal-Mart did, a lot of suffering we had had to endure would not have happened.

Evacuations of the Superdome and Convention Center were slow to get started. Shelters opened all across Louisiana to provide housing for those being evacuated and fleeing New Orleans. Eventually, 193 shelter locations in Louisiana alone became home to over 44,400 evacuees. This number did not include evacuees who were staying with family and friends. Governmental services were stretched to the limit in every town and city in the state.

Within hours of the floodwaters overwhelming New Orleans, on August 30, Baton Rouge city officials turned over the keys to the River Center, an indoor arena and convention center on the banks of the Mississippi River. Within days, the population shot up to 6,720 evacuees. Some 40 miles west, in the City of Lafayette, the Cajun Dome arena housed more than 6,000 evacuees, along with the health care services required to care for the many health challenges created by the evacuees. Examination rooms and a huge pharmacy were set up to attend to the evacuees.

Lafayette Police Sergeant Kelly Gibson explained the security concerns associated with running a shelter where thousands would show up with only a few possessions. Working the intake portion of the Cajun Dome at around 3:00 A.M., a petite woman in her fifties came into the shelter with her mother and son. She pulled Sergeant Gibson aside and opened the suitcase to show that it was overstuffed with cash. She said she was a bar owner and that she was fleeing her flooded home in New Orleans. He told her he couldn't guarantee the safety of her money if she kept it in the shelter. With a voice full of confidence and cockiness, she told Sergeant Gibson, "Mister, I don't want you to hold my money. I just want you to know I got it in case someone tries to take it and I stop them." Gazing around the masses of bags and suitcases countless evacuees were clinging to, he wondered with great concern about the potential security risk.

Finally back from Reno, Nevada, Lieutenants Pam Schmitt and Pam Negrotto reported for duty. Also, Lori Duplessis, Susie Breaux, a community programs officer in the Special Services Division, and my secretary, Michelle Oncale, had all returned from being evacuated. All five, with the assistance of Corporal Hebert, prepared to open a shelter for visiting law enforcement personnel.

With power restored at Destrehan High School, located on the east bank of St. Charles Parish, it had been selected as a police shelter for its two air-conditioned gyms, complete with shower facilities. This would allow one gym to be used as a day shift dorm and the other for night shift, causing as little disruption as possible to our sleeping volunteers. The police shelter at Harry Hurst Middle School was still without power and occupied by St. Charles Parish Deputies; it was closed, and the displaced deputies were moved to Destrehan High School as well. The Special Services Division crew wasted no time in getting the shelter operational and ready for the volunteers who were expected to begin arriving the next day.

St. Charles Parish Hospital needed their bed space, and the 28 rescued from the Convention Center who had spent the night there needed to find alternative housing. I readied the lobby of the storm damaged Special Services Building, using a small air conditioner, with plans to run power from the main generator that supplied the St. Charles Emergency

Operation Center. It wouldn't be needed. Before nightfall, all but the Australians had been reunited with family members. The Australians stayed with Sheriff Champagne and his wife, Alice, until a return flight home could be arranged.

Making a pass by St. Charles Parish Hospital, I met with Sergeants Lebeauf and LaGrange. The hospital had since resumed operations and had quickly been overwhelmed. Most hospitals in the Greater New Orleans area were flooded, making St. Charles Parish Hospital one of the few operational healthcare facilities in the region. Evacuees had swarmed the building. To deal with the influx, a strict access procedure was set in place, and a single entrance was established. Minutes before I arrived, staff had scared off a group of about 15 people with questionable intentions who were trying to access the building through the loading docks. Pulling more people in for security, the hospital was locked down tight and a credentialing process put in place.

A shining example of teamwork surfaced and helped Hurricane Katrina's victims with desperately needed information, both at home and abroad. Entercom Communications and Clear Channel Radio, two rivals in the radio media industry, formed the United Radio Broadcasters of New Orleans. It made perfect sense. Both owned several radio stations in the New Orleans Metro Area, both had suffered major destruction to the facilities and towers, and both needed to get back on the air to provide vital information to those trapped on a roof, or in evacuation shelters and hotels hundreds of miles away.

Sharing studio space and equipment, familiar voices from several stations were paired off in teams. Radio personalities from hip hop stations sat next to deejays from country music stations; deejays from rock music stations sat next to deejays from talk/news stations. With one united voice transmitting on radio stations in five states and over the Internet, they did much to calm the residents of southeast Louisiana and southern Mississippi and provide them with important information, 24 hours a day.

I found this amusing. Rival companies and deejays that seemingly would have very little in common were able to work effectively together towards one common goal: serving the people in a ravaged region. But, for some reason, local, state and federal government couldn't do the same. Mayor Nagin seemed to be in a power struggle with Governor Blanco, both Democrats. Governor Blanco seemed unwilling or unable to coordinate efforts with the Republican White House. Rather than put politics aside and help people in desperate need, a sluggish response created by poor planning kept getting worse and creating even more senseless suffering.

Louisiana Fraternal Order of Police members Johnny Frederic and Tommy Tizzard were back in action. The day before, during their trip into New Orleans to drop off Deputy Balser to retrieve his police car, they had spoken to several New Orleans Police officers, Jefferson Parish deputies, and Crescent City Connection Police officers. All had the same request: they needed ammo, and lots of it. Back in Gonzales, the pair visited businesses and bought supplies to deliver on their return trip. They pulled into the Park Place Nightclub, the owner of which Johnny Frederic knew. With the intent of emptying his icemaker into several ice chests and in their rush to get the supplies to those who needed it, Frederic failed to notice construction activity near the nightclub. Unaware that a contractor had just poured concrete on the side of the building, Frederic drove right through it. They all thought it was amusing, but the poor guy finishing the cement found no humor in the situation. Using good judgment, they promptly left.

Chest Deep and Rising:

They were headed back to the city with $5,000.00 worth of assorted ammo. The pair brought with them an additional treat, which some commented was the best meal they had ever eaten. Before leaving Baton Rouge with the ammo, they stopped at Kentucky Fried Chicken and bought every piece of fried chicken they could get their hands on. Kentucky Fried Chicken might not seem like a gourmet meal, but for guys who hadn't eaten hot food in days, you would have thought it was the very finest cuisine.

Johnny Frederic and Tommy Tizzard commented that when they went into Jefferson Parish, it was as if what they first saw was so bad they could not believe it would get worse... but it did. They turned off on Williams Boulevard onto Veterans Boulevard in Kenner, Louisiana. On a normal day, there was so much traffic you had to pay attention and move quickly to get where you needed to be. On that day, they were the only traffic! The area was deserted, with the exception of a few people going in and out of the broken glass doors of businesses: looters or survivors, call them what you will. The highways were riddled with wood, stone, litter and power lines. The buildings had been blown out and down and in half. The façades of buildings had been blow off, or the roofs were gone. Some buildings were just skeletons of iron, where debris had accumulated and become trapped and snarled and entangled as it tried to escape. Cars were overturned, some on their sides. Strange things were seen everywhere, like the roof on the Blockbuster Video store had been torn off, but the awning over the sidewalk seemed to be untouched.

They arrived at the Four Points Sheraton on Veterans Boulevard at I-10 in Metairie. There they saw several Jefferson Parish deputies, most of whom Tommy Tizzard had worked with for many years. The deputies looked like the area: rattled and in disarray. They had taken over the hotel and were working and sleeping there. There was no electricity, the temperature and humidity were both in the high 90s, and there was no running water. The deputies were using the swimming pool to bathe and cool off, and flushing the toilets by dipping out buckets of water from the pool.

They made their rounds, dropped off the ammo and food and took orders from law enforcement members. The biggest request was for fresh underwear and personal hygiene products, big and small, for males and females. Many officers were left with only the clothes on their back as Katrina had destroyed their homes. After several days in the sweltering heat and no fresh water to wash, you can certainly understand the request. After dropping off their load at various agencies, it was back to Baton Rouge, where they bought truckloads of underwear, deodorant, waterless soap, toothbrushes and toothpaste, and the like.

A Time of Anger

I began planning a return trip to the Convention Center to look for the luggage discarded the night before. Major John Cornwell, who had worked on a rotating shift with others as the law enforcement coordinator in the St. Charles Emergency Operations Center, mentioned that he, too, wished to go to the Convention Center. Together with Captain Walsdorf, Lieutenant Lee and others, off we went. When we arrived at the location where we had parked the bus the night before, I was devastated to see that the contents of the bags had been strewn across the curb. I searched endlessly for the jewelry, but it was long gone. We did pick up a number of personal papers we found and later returned them to one of the nurses.

What a difference a day makes! The scene had changed at the Convention Center. The thugs were gone. A larger contingent of National Guard troops was now stationed at various locations around the Convention Center. The parking lot that had separated the school bus and the thugs the night before was now a heliport used by numerous helicopters, with long, orderly lines of evacuees awaiting their flight to freedom. Major Cornwell's reason for wanting to go to the Convention Center was of personal importance to him; and for me, it was an eye-opening experience. His brother works in New Orleans, not far from the Convention Center, and his family had not heard from him since before the storm. On foot, Major Cornwell and I walked the entire quarter-mile length of the 1.2 million square feet convention facility. Through the crowds, the rubbish, rubble, human feces, and revolting smells, we walked, armed with assault rifles, calling out the name Michael Cornwell, and searching.

The experience not only upset me, but I found myself becoming increasingly furious with every step. The day before, it had been easy to think that the vast majority of the people at the Convention Center were out-of-control thugs. While clearly there had been thugs preying on the masses, that percentage was very small. The overwhelming majority were good, honest people caught in a really bad situation. They had been routed to the Convention Center by a twist of fate beyond their control. They came from hospitals, nursing homes, and hotels, all under the guise that buses would be waiting to take them to safety. Each day, they were told buses were on their way, a phrase repeated for four long, hot days. How long would I allow my family to be subjected to such deplorable conditions? These people were lied to by their local, state, and federal government—not on purpose, but through a lack of competence at all levels.

About midway through our walk of the Convention Center, I stopped to talk to a New Orleans Police officer. He explained to me that he had been on site the entire time, living in a police car. He had lost his home in the Lakeview area. With no communications, he was left to fend for himself. I asked if we could get anything for him and bring it in the next day. He thanked me, but said that hopefully he would be moving to another location. The National Guard expected to have the site evacuated in less than 24 hours. I explained that we were looking for a family member. With a look that suggested we had a better chance of winning the lottery, he said, "Good luck!"

He explained to us how people at the Convention Center had basically segregated themselves into three distinct groups, and depending on where you were dropped off played a big part of how you fared in such an environment. At the north end, near Julia Street, were the elderly and their caregivers. There were few problems with this crowd, but they were the most vulnerable to the elements. At the south end were the thugs (where we had rescued the nurses the night before). They were criminals who had terrorized their own neighborhoods before Hurricane Katrina; only now they were in concentrated numbers, fighting for control. In between the two groups were the families with children. They, too, had considerable medical needs, but were orderly. He explained how the thugs would roam through the entire crowd at night, preying on the innocent and weak. I thanked him, wished him luck, and we went on searching for Michael Cornwell. I couldn't help thinking what a hero this man was.

As we walked, people approached us, asking for help. Many carried babies, some thanking us for finally sending help;

others, with fearful expressions, asked if we were going to leave at nightfall. Towards the north end of the Convention Center, my anger grew even further. Elderly men and women lined the curb, as if they were still in the same position in which they had been dropped off. How could something like this happen in America? My only comfort was that you could see progress; National Guard Troops were everywhere, and buses and helicopters were rapidly taking people out of the city. There was finally progress, and not a moment too soon. I doubt many of these people could have survived much longer.

Reaching Julia Street, we were unsuccessful in locating Major Cornwell's brother. We tried to walk inside the Convention Center itself, but the stench and heat had forced everyone outside, where an occasional breeze provided some relief. Walking was a challenge—that is, if you did not want to step in human waste. Conditions for the entire quarter-mile were absolutely disgusting. The things that are still etched in my mind are the smells, the multiple bullet holes in the glass overhang, the piles of trash filled with silver platters, flat screen televisions, and china. I am sure these were items that had meant a great deal to someone early on in this ordeal, but at some point, survival rendered these items of little value. But perhaps the one image I think I will never forget is that of the elderly, sitting helplessly on the curb, waiting for someone, anyone, to help them.

Assessing our next step, a decision was made that some in the group would continue on and again attempt to reach St. Bernard Parish, to give Lieutenant Lee an opportunity to assess the damage to his flooded home while Major Cornwell, Captain Walsdorf and myself would return to St. Charles Parish. With the back of the Durango filled and three seats already taken, Major Cornwell approached the crowd near Julia Street, and asked if anyone had a place in the River Parishes they could go to. One lady stepped forward, saying she had family in Laplace, LA, just west of St. Charles Parish. We loaded her and her bags into the Durango and we were off to Laplace. Major Cornwell later learned that his brother's family had safely evacuated to Houston, after spending a week living in a warehouse near Charity Hospital in New Orleans.

After reuniting the lady with her family, we went back to the St. Charles Parish Courthouse to retrieve our police cars. I made a pass by the public shelter at Eual J. Landry Middle School, then the hospital, to see how things were progressing. Then I was off to my house. Listening to WWL Radio on the drive home, it amazed me how much disconnect there was in communications on all levels. I had watched images of the Superdome and Convention Center on the Sheriff's satellite TV the day before, so I could not understand the reports I was listening to. Homeland Security Secretary Chertoff was quoted as saying he had not heard a report of thousands of people at the Convention Center who didn't have food and water. FEMA Director Brown was also telling reporters that he had just learned of the Convention Center situation. I couldn't help thinking they should take some of the billions of dollars in relief aid, a phrase they kept throwing around in conversations as their response to the region, and spend a few dollars on a subscription to the Dish Network. Then they could hire someone who could watch it, to let them know what was going on.

Walking into my home around 11:00 P.M., I sat on the sofa in the living room, answered a few questions from my wife, Gail, about the day's activities, and commented on going to top off the fuel tanks of the generator. Gail laughed and asked if I had noticed the streetlights on outside. The power to my area had been restored. I was so angry and tired, I hadn't even noticed.

PART TWO

Day Eight
Friday, September 2, 2005

Post-Katrina Evacuation Intensifies

In the early morning hours of Friday, September 2nd, a frantic Sergeant Patrick Theriot of the Crescent City Connection Police Department, with jurisdiction of a high-rise bridge crossing above the Mississippi River in New Orleans, called Johnny Frederic on his cell phone and woke him from the few hours of sleep he had gotten in days. Johnny Frederic was at his St. Amant, Louisiana home and outside the crippled 504 telephone exchange, which severely hampered the ability to successfully make local calls. Stationed atop the main travel lanes of the bridge and unable to make contact with anyone locally by either radio or cell phone, Sergeant Theriot advised Johnny Frederic that a chemical plant had just exploded on the west bank of New Orleans, and he asked that the fire department be notified. The powerful blast itself had already made notification. Rumors that the chemical cloud produced by the explosion was toxic were later determined not to be credible, but nonetheless, it created even greater chaos in an already tense atmosphere. It was to be a tense start to yet another bad day.

In the Superdome and Convention Center, progress was being made in the evacuation efforts, but it was a slow, complex process. It wasn't as easy as simply arranging buses to transport 50 people per bus away from the flooded city. First, a final destination had to be arranged, with adequate facilities and resources to handle the large number of people, many with special needs. Although evacuees were being displaced to nearly every state, Texas, with an estimated 250,000 evacuees, and more specifically the City of Houston, would be the recipient of the vast number of the displaced Louisianans. When the Texas Fire Marshal declared the Houston Astrodome to be at capacity, the Reliant Center, also in Houston, was opened as an evacuee shelter. It, too, would soon fill to capacity.

Even with these important issues addressed, surprisingly, getting people onto the buses would prove to be a challenge. In the chaos present at both the Superdome and Convention Center, family members had a difficult time staying together, and would hold up the bus departure by refusing to board until their entire family was together. To speed things up, quick-thinking New Orleans Police officers devised a system that streamlined the process. With barricades, they created multiple staging areas, into which 50 people would enter. Once in a staging area, if members of the group had wandered off, the next, intact staged group was escorted to an awaiting bus. This not only streamlined the process, but it also allowed more than just the very front of the line to see progress. It calmed tempers as well.

With evacuation shelters in Louisiana and Texas filled to capacity, additional shelters were needed. To accommodate this demand, states all across the US offered to establish shelters. Getting evacuees to these shelters would be challenging. Again catching off guard the limited numbers of Jefferson

Chest Deep and Rising:

Parish Sheriff's deputies providing security at the airport, buses loaded with evacuees began arriving at the airport.

The confusion and frustration of all at the airport caused a very tense atmosphere. With Concourse D still being used as a triage area for medical evacuations, the remaining areas of the airport quickly became over-burdened with evacuees. Still without full electrical power and a functional sewage system, the estimated 27,000 people passing through the airport created deplorable conditions, which, under normal circumstances, would have caused the airport facility to be condemned as a health hazard. Nonetheless, evacuees arrived by the busload and left by the planeload.

To expedite the process, evacuees were escorted onto planes without knowing their intended destination. Their names were recorded as they boarded the plane and, upon landing, they were provided tickets that brought them to their assigned cities with shelters. Confusion was caused by attempting to keep families together. This, along with not being able to identify evacuees' final destinations, caused hostilities to rise.

Also placing demands on the Jefferson deputies was the fact that people who had evacuated their homes took with them many possessions, some of which were weapons. Aware that they would be required to pass through metal detectors and security screenings before boarding the planes, weapons were being discarded throughout the airport property, posing a serious safety risk.

With such a poorly executed plan causing suffering, someone had to be at fault, and the Congressional Black Caucus, along with the NAACP, Black Leadership Forum, and the National Urban League, focused their anger over the sluggish relief efforts squarely on the President, citing the poverty level of the residents of New Orleans as a primary reason for the delay.

That same morning, President Bush toured Alabama, Mississippi and Louisiana to get a firsthand look at Hurricane Katrina's damage. He described the relief efforts up to that point as "not acceptable," and authorized the dispatch of 7,200 active-duty ground troops to the area—the first major commitment of regular ground forces in the crisis. The Pentagon announced that an additional 10,000 National Guard troops would be deployed to Louisiana and Mississippi, raising the total Guard contingent to about 40,000.

Back in St. Charles Parish, leaders were preparing to make decisions that would not only facilitate the rebound locally, but in the entire region. One thing St. Charles Parish had going in its favor was the lack of widespread flooding. With most of the floodwaters pumped out of the levee systems, the majority of the St. Charles Parish's infrastructure remained intact. This meant that St. Charles Parish was in the best location and condition to serve as a staging area for the growing number of services needed throughout the affected region. With the virtual shutdown of all commerce, products and goods normally available to the general public were quickly dwindling. In addition, there was the need to restart many of the industrial complexes in St. Charles Parish that supply energy resources to much of the United States.

During a time when Jefferson and Orleans officials were demanding their parishes be shut down for a suggested month before anyone could return, St. Charles Parish would soon begin encouraging its residents to come home, to begin the process of putting their lives back together and offering support to its neighboring parishes.

Make it Happen

The toughest part of solving any problem, regardless of how complex or how simple, is committing to do it. Once committed, everything seems to fall in place. After days of hearing promises from state and federal officials that help and much-needed resources were on the way, and defying directives from FEMA calling for prior approval—an approval process that in itself seems to be its own disaster area—we had had enough. St. Charles officials chose to aggressively address the challenges facing the area on their own, and figure out how to pay the bills later.

At the 9:00 A.M. briefing at the St. Charles Emergency Operations Center, department heads were faced with many issues, all of which would have made it easy to justify the need for a little more time before committing, yet each worked collectively. Emergency Operations Director Tab Troxler went around the table, encouraging department and agency representatives to identify their immediate problems and concerns about opening St. Charles Parish. He also challenged everyone present to work collectively to resolve each issue. "Make it happen!", a phrase used frequently during the early discussions in this meeting, would quickly become the motto and, ultimately, the attitude of everyone in St. Charles Parish following Hurricane Katrina. Like a finely tuned engine, everyone and every agency worked efficiently and effectively towards one common goal: bringing St. Charles Parish residents home. In a time when state and federal assistance appeared to be overburdened and less than adequate in their response, this was a refreshing change and a boost in morale.

The first challenge was dealing with Jefferson Parish President Aaron Broussard's decision to shut down Jefferson Parish to all residents. With 453,000 residents in Jefferson Parish alone, the sheer volume of traffic trying to return was demanding. Broussard, at times, seemed out of control, with his excited description of the destruction experienced in Jefferson Parish. At a time when storm victims were looking for a calm voice of control and reassurance from their public officials, Jefferson Parish residents had little to find comfort in.

The cause of flooding in Jefferson Parish would be different than in Orleans, Plaquemines, St. Bernard, and St. Tammany Parishes. In each of those parishes, tidal surges either breached or overtopped levees. In Jefferson, rainwater trapped by the very levees that protected them from tidal surge was the culprit. Jefferson Parish President Aaron Broussard had made a conscious decision before Hurricane Katrina's arrival—a decision so controversial that it ignited a political storm the winds of Hurricane Katrina. He chose to move his pump operators to higher ground during the storm, outside of Jefferson Parish. Because of this, drainage pumps were not operational and failed to pump out rainwater as it fell. To make matter even worse, tidal surge flowed back through the idle pumps adding to the rising water levels in the Jefferson Parish. Water naturally seeks out low elevations, which caused extensive flooding. His argument about protecting life before property was silenced when scores of other public employees remained on the job throughout the storm, over 1,000 of which were with the Jefferson Parish Sheriff's Office.

Days earlier, Broussard had announced that Jefferson Parish would remain completely shut down to all traffic except emergency vehicles, something he had wavered on frequently in the preceding days. This caused the St. Charles

Parish Sheriff's Office many challenges. Bordering parishes to the west of St. Charles Parish decided to remove their traffic control points. With Interstate 10 closed by flooding and a levee constructed across US Highway 61 at the St. Charles Parish line, this created a parking lot effect on US Highway 90. Since Highway 90 was the only functional access to the region, this decision seriously hindered relief supplies and emergency vehicle access to the New Orleans Metro Area.

Broussard's never-ending access exceptions, not to mention the issuance of a seemingly endless number of access permits he offered on-line, created horrendous traffic congestion. By allowing residents to return home in St. Charles Parish, it made it much easier to manage the traffic concerns in the remote area of the St. Charles and Jefferson Parish line on the west bank.

A 24-hour presence was established, port-a-lets and lighting plants were deployed, and Sheriff's personnel were assigned to maintain not only a traffic check point, but patrol the shoulders of the highway where people from Jefferson Parish wishing to return home began erecting tents as their cars sat in line on the highway. They did so in anticipation of a chance to slip into Jefferson Parish during the frequent exceptions Broussard had demonstrated, as he often changed his orders. Although demanding for weeks to come, the problem was solved.

But this wouldn't be the end of the challenges facing St. Charles Parish. The lack of full electrical power restoration caused concerns that sewage lift stations would not be operational and could cause systems to back up into open drainage ditches and homes. Add to this the issues existing with the east bank water treatment plant, which was running at only partial capacity. Notices would be issued to returning residents regarding a need to conserve water, and that a failure to do so could result in a disruption in water services. A plan to deploy generators and pump trucks to various sewage lift stations on a regular schedule was devised to alleviate the potential for back flow, and these problems also were solved.

With communications still fractured throughout the region, the use of credit and debit cards was nonexistent. Banks needed to open to allow customers and businesses the ability to get cash. Security systems at banks and stores were nonfunctional. This would require law enforcement personnel to be assigned to all banks, and the larger stores in the parish. Wal-Mart wanted to open its doors to the public, but due to the lack of employees and security systems, they limited the customers who could enter the store at any given time. Each was only allowed to purchase a limited number of items per visit. The real challenge resulted in the sheer volume of customers. Literally, a thousand people would stand in lines daily, exposed to the brutal sun, for a remote chance of getting needed items. As assisting law enforcement and national guardsmen arrived, extra personnel would be assigned to the stores and banks as needed. Another problem solved.

Many of the petrochemical plants needed more security. They lacked their own security personnel due to evacuations. Evacuated production employees were watching television reports of lawlessness in New Orleans on television from their remote locations. It was difficult, therefore, for company officials to encourage their critical staff to return to work. The promise of special access passes, on-site housing, and heightened security at the facilities seemed to calm fears. Another problem solved.

Entergy Power Company needed to reestablish power connectivity at a power facility in Westwego, located in Jefferson Parish, known as "Nine Mile Point." However, the power crews had fled the area the day before because of reports that they were being shot at by people in the neighborhood. These claims were never substantiated, but the perception was that it wasn't safe, and that became the reality of most work crews during the initial days. The repair work at Nine Mile Point was critical to reestablishing the St. Charles Parish power grid. Unable to secure assistance from an overburdened Jefferson Parish Sheriff's Office, St. Charles deputies accompanied the power crew.

Although each challenge seemed to have a solution, all of this was not without a price. Nearly every challenge required the deployment of law enforcement personnel. As law enforcement volunteers arrived, they were assigned to posts on rotating shifts and allowed the plan to take effect. Thus the recovery of St. Charles Parish had begun. Calls were made to the media, encouraging St. Charles residents to return home, beginning Saturday morning. They were encouraged to be prepared by bringing supplies for several days, and told that there would be restrictions on water consumption and they should anticipate a lack of available services.

Just a few miles away, things were drastically different. St. Bernard Parish, on the southeast side of New Orleans, Plaquemines Parish, parts of St. Tammany Parish, all of the Mississippi Gulf Coast and all of New Orleans were still in a vulnerable state, even though conditions were improving. Finally, supplies and support began to trickle in. The level of destruction was enormous. As St. Charles Parish began picking up the pieces, these areas were still in search-and-rescue mode.

Friday evening, after setting up duty assignments and ensuring that arriving volunteers would be processed and cared for, a group of deputies, including myself, ventured into New Orleans and met up with Johnny Frederic and retired Gonzales Police Chief, Pete Burque, to spend the day delivering supplies and ammo to officers in the worst-impacted areas. They attempted to make it to St. Bernard Parish, but were turned around by floodwaters. They visited Plaquemines Parish and made contact with Colonel Charles Guey, someone I had tried to call many times, unsuccessfully. He and members of his department had safely ridden out the storm in Belle Chase, but two-thirds of his parish was still underwater from a 25-foot tidal surge that had toppled their levees system.

Passing on the elevated portions of Interstate 10, rising 30 feet above the city, we were in awe of the widespread devastation and floodwaters. At the Superdome, thousands of people were still standing outside the Dome terrace. Helicopters filled the air as they carried large sandbags to drop in levee breaches, large water bags to release on structure fires, and rescue baskets could occasionally be seen, plucking people from rooftops. Our first stop in New Orleans was the Canal Street entrance of Harrah's Casino, Louisiana's only land-based casino, located on high ground only a block from the Mississippi River.

The New Orleans Police Department had set up a makeshift command post after floodwaters inundated police headquarters about a mile away. I wanted to find someone who could assist us in assessing the needs of the officers so we could focus our support efforts on their particular needs. After walking around the covered entrance of the casino, looking for someone, anyone, who appeared in charge, we gave up. We decided our efforts would best be focused on making contact with the officers in each district. But with 80% of New Orleans under water, it was difficult to determine the location of where each district had moved.

New Orleans Police Department's First District Station was one of the only districts still in its station buildings, and it just happened to be on our list of places to visit. Captain Walsdorf's niece, Officer Athena Monteleone, was assigned to that district. Night had begun to fall in the city. With the power out, visibility faded quickly. Standing water and debris blocking roadways made maneuvering through the city a challenge. Captain Walsdorf, Lieutenant Lee, and I turned onto Rampart Street and drove towards the First District Station. With police strobe lights on to announce our arrival, two well-armed officers, who had established a secure perimeter around the station, quickly met us. Staring down their rifle barrels as they stood in a ready position, I stopped abruptly. Unable to see inside my police car, due to the blinding strobes, and with the rumors that police cars were being stolen in the city, they were taking no chances, and I didn't blame them one bit. I slowly exited my car and was immediately recognized; they lowered their rifles and clicked them back onto safety. We talked to the armed officers for a while before proceeding into the station.

Located in the first floor parking area of the station, a large group of officers were resting and getting a bite to eat. Many were dressed in civilian clothing, with badges pinned to their shirts and the holsters and sidearm strapped to their sides. Most had discarded their uniforms earlier after being in them for days, wading through contaminated water. Some carried a shotgun or a rifle as if it were an extension of their bodies. They looked exhausted, yet upbeat. They seemed to be very excited to have someone visit their station and in true southern hospitality style, they offered us their food, something to drink, a place to sit and talk for a while. As much as the delivery of supplies was important and necessary to these officers, who seemed to have been cut off from any logistical support from their own police department, there was an additional need. These officers just wanted to talk. They didn't want to talk to just anyone. They wanted to explain what they were forced to deal with to someone who walks in their own shoes and would understand. It was important to them that people knew they were still on the job.

First District Commander Captain Jimmy Scott arrived as we were leaving, as did Walsdorf's niece, Athena. Her hand was securely wrapped in a bandage after receiving a pretty nasty dog bite. Captain Walsdorf and a very emotional Athena walked off to an unoccupied corner of the station to talk, for seeing a family member for the first time since the storm was an overwhelming experience.

Captain Scott explained the many challenges his district was facing. He advised that the district's location, on the outside edge of the French Quarter and partially surrounded by floodwater, actually assisted in its security at night. With the city in total darkness, sentries placed on the roof of the district station needed only to watch the still water at the base of the building. Any activity would create a ripple effect on the water's surface, which would lead directly to the cause of the disturbance. He also explained the efforts by his officers to protect the New Orleans French Quarter. The historic heart of the city had suffered wind and rain damage, but no significant flooding. The Quarter's buildings, dating back to 1718, are arranged in a 70-block area. With fire protection hampered, a single structure fire could wipe out the entire historic district and with it, much of the economic engine that drives the city's tourism-based economy. Captain Scott was determined to make sure this did not happen.

As I drove back home that night, I couldn't help wondering: if these officers were this isolated from support and supplies and were still located in their district buildings, what could be expected of the other districts, having been forced to relocate to various locations throughout the city?

Day Nine
Saturday, September 3, 2005

Despair Gives Way to Progress

Saturday, September 3rd started with tragedy. St. Charles Deputies were dispatched to the parking lot of Sal's Restaurant, a popular St. Charles Parish restaurant located on US Hwy 90 in Boutte, LA. There they made a disturbing discovery. Seated in the front seat of an unmarked Ford Taurus that displayed a public license plate was the lifeless body of a 36-year-old man dressed in a New Orleans Police Department uniform, the result of an apparent self-inflicted gunshot wound. The body was identified as New Orleans Police Officer Paul Accardo, who had apparently become overwhelmed and distraught with the hellish environment that had overcome his city. On his way to a family member's home in nearby Terrebonne Parish, he apparently pulled into the restaurant parking lot, where he ended his life. Earlier that same day, another New Orleans Police Officer had done the same. Officer Larry Celestine, assigned to the Seventh District of the New Orleans Police Department, also perished from an apparent self-inflicted gunshot wound. The stress placed on the officers in such a volatile environment was never more evident.

At the Louisiana Fraternal Order of Police office in Baton Rouge, calls poured in from all across America, many wanting to offer assistance, financially and through donated supplies. My wife, Gail, would drive to Baton Rouge each day for the next few weeks to help Jimmy Gallagher, a retired New Orleans Police Officer, and State Lodge Treasurer. Together with Nancy and Julie Tizzard, Tommy's wife and daughter, they helped coordinate relief efforts, record messages, and run the state office. Claude Schlesinger, a retired New Orleans Police Officer and Louisiana State Lodge General Legal Counsel, also set up shop in the office and offered legal services to members in need. Claude's home had flooded and his New Orleans office, located on the 25th floor of the Entergy Building, was inaccessible due to flooding.

Repeated calls from New Orleans Police Officers Art Bancroft and Louie Gaydosh demonstrated the frustrations created by a fractured communications network and the determination of officers to return to the flooded city to help in the rescue and recovery efforts.

Officer Gaydosh reported for duty prior to the storm striking. He worked during and through the storm only to find his home in the Lakeview area of the city had flooded. Officer Gaydosh was in charge of a Ryder rental truck which had been commandeered by Officer Mike Hunter, a resourceful 7th District police officer. Together, with Officer Hunter driving and Officer Gaydosh literally riding shotgun, they transported rescued citizens from several pickup points on Chef Menteur Highway to the Convention Center. In the days that followed, they met with a Ryder dealer in Algiers who presented them with two more trucks to use in the rescue efforts.

When Gaydosh was given the opportunity to take a five day furlough, he reunited with his family who evacuated to Houston. While driving through Baton Rouge, Gaydosh was contacted by Arthur Bancroft who was on a cruise ship departing from Boston en route to Canada. Bancroft flew to Houston were the two officers met. Together, they would drive back to New Orleans.

While in Houston, Gaydosh contacted the Harris County Fraternal Order of Police Lodge and met with Detective Chuck Leithner of the Harris County Sheriff's Office. Explaining their situation, Detective Leithner took them to several businesses in the Houston area that provided much-needed ammunition and police supplies that the pair of officers would bring back to New Orleans.

After a stop in Lafayette, Louisiana to purchase a handgun for Bancroft at a police equipment store and an overnight stop for food, supplies, and rest at the Baton Rouge Fraternal Order of Police Lodge, they again hit the road and drove back into New Orleans where they resumed their police duties.

Many of the calls received at the State Lodge Office were from police officers from all parts of the United States, who wished to open their homes to police families. A running list of the offers was created. This caused a real concern. There was no doubt that the offers were sincere, but by publicizing these well-intended offers, we would be facilitating the departure of experienced officers from local agencies that were already in desperate need. Instead, when a local officer would call, seeking assistance for their family members relocated to other states, the list was used to provide support to evacuating family members.

Having witnessed the conditions of the officers in the areas with the greatest impact, the Fraternal Order of Police would increase its efforts in supplying the officers who, with the loss of their homes, had nothing to wear but the clothes they had reported to duty with. Blue t-shirts with "POLICE" written in large white letters on the front and back were ordered. I couldn't help wondering if the media reports of diminished police presence were actually due to their lack of visibility caused by the abandonment of contaminated uniforms. Almost immediately, thanks to a local screen-printing business in Baton Rouge and a National Fraternal Order of Police vendor, t-shirts were produced and delivered to the State Lodge Office in Baton Rouge. Johnny Frederic, Tommy Tizzard, retired Gonzales Chief Pete Bourque, and Gonzales Constable Steve Juneau loaded their truck and increased delivery supply efforts.

Joining the Fraternal Order of Police delivery crew, we started making a list of the temporary district locations. Every officer we saw on the street, we would stop, offer ammunition and supplies, and ask where the temporary district locations were. It was amazing how little information each district had regarding the location and the condition of their counterparts within the same department. It was as if each district was in its own world, working independently of each other, each carrying out rescue and patrol missions directed by district commanders on their own. Despite this breakdown in communications and organizational leadership and lack of resources, each district I visited was operating in a highly efficient manner. They initiated rescue and patrol operations with the limited resources at their disposal and with a prioritized plan; every member of each district had their responsibilities. At nightfall, however, with no means of communicating other than line of sight, with few exceptions all officers returned to their districts.

One thing that did hamper each district was the mass dissemination of false information. Rumors and greatly exaggerated stories were reported as factual. The communications

Chest Deep and Rising:

infrastructure was so fractured that Mayor Nagin and New Orleans Police Superintendent Eddie Compass were confirming reports of murders and rapes in the Louisiana Superdome and Convention Center, which would later be unsubstantiated. These reports were not limited to the Superdome and Convention Center alone. Rumors included gun battles, anticipated death tolls numbering 40,000, shooting at rescue helicopters and, stranded on overpasses, people dying by the hundreds from a lack of water and food. Each report took on a life of it's own. From the mayor to the reporter, from the officer on the street to people across the globe watching events unfold on television, perception became reality.

By Saturday evening, however, for the first time since Katrina arrived, progress was visible. By that afternoon alone, 42,000 people had been evacuated from New Orleans. Evacuation efforts were shifted to the Convention Center, where the last 1,500 were also being evacuated. A hospital ship arrived and the announcement that a cruise ship was on its way to provide temporary housing for first responders did much to lift spirits.

After dropping off all our supplies in New Orleans, we attempted to make it to St. Bernard Parish. With floodwaters still too high, St. Bernard would remain cut off for yet another day. With night falling quickly, we headed back home to regroup. Johnny Frederic went shopping in Baton Rouge for the next day's supplies, and I returned to the police shelter at Destrehan High School to see how things were progressing. With a few visiting officers beginning to arrive, the shelter crew assigned to oversee the facility had arranged themselves on rotating shifts. As officers arrived, they were processed, provided the oath of office and, based on their scheduled shift assignment, they were assigned to the appropriate gym used as a dormitory.

Standing in the school parking lot, I stopped to talk with Corpus Christi Port Authority Officer Ken Starrs, the National Trustee on the Fraternal Order of Police board from Texas. Ken had just completed a shift at the traffic checkpoint on US Hwy 61. He had a few days off work and, after seeing my email requesting assistance, he had wanted to drive in and help during his off days. We shared our storm experiences; I thanked him for his help and went home for the night.

A Rearranged World Emerges

Hurricane Katrina drastically changed many lives in ways that would have seemed extreme before the storm. In the case of the Chaisson family of Destrehan, Louisiana, their family crises would take on a special challenge. Hurricane Katrina had rearranged their world.

Mrs. Goldie G. Gulledge, the 91-year-old grandmother of Louisiana State Senator Joel Chaisson II, had passed away at St. Charles Specialty Hospital only hours before Hurricane Katrina made her arrival. Saint Charles Specialty Hospital, located on St. Charles Avenue in New Orleans, would later be the location of many horror stories reported to have occurred in this evacuated hospital alone before, during, and immediately following Hurricane Katrina. Wishing to retrieve the body for a proper burial and unable to make contact with anyone at the abandoned hospital, the Chaisson family turned to Sheriff Champagne and Dr. Brian Brogle, the St. Charles Parish Coroner, for assistance.

After several attempts to make contact with hospital representatives, Sheriff Champagne sent deputies to accompany Dr. Brogle and Coroner Investigator Craig Melancon on

Saturday evening, as they drove to St. Charles Specialty Hospital with the hope of making contact with a hospital representative in person. Lieutenants Rodney Madere and Ricky Oubre, Dr. Brogle, and Investigator Melancon departed in an ambulance and an unmarked police car. On the way, they were amazed by the number of homes in non-flooded portions of New Orleans with doors kicked in and windows busted, the apparent result of burglaries and looting. As they got closer to the hospital, they were forced to drive through water two feet deep. When they parked in front of the hospital, people immediately began approaching them. Concerned that these people may be armed, they ordered the people to stay away. They found the hospital completely abandoned, with all doors locked. They were afraid that their vehicles might be stolen if they left them unattended and entered the hospital to search for the body, and so decided to leave.

With a better plan, a new day, and more help, a second attempt was made to retrieve Mrs. Gulledge's body by Lieutenants Madere, Mark Candies, and Billy LeBlanc, along with Dr. Brogle, Officers Jeff Duplessis, Jerry Murphy, John Olszowka, and Josh Cuthcart, volunteers from out-of-state agencies, and State Senator Joel Chaisson. The group traveled in two pick-up trucks and a Crime Scene van. Arriving at the hospital, they forced the front doors open with a crowbar and a sledgehammer. Lieutenants Madere and Leblanc, Dr. Brogle and two other officers entered the hospital, while the others remained outside, protecting the vehicles from possible looters. Dr. Brogle had been informed that Mrs. Gulledge's body would be in the Emergency Room.

The hospital was completely dark, except near windows. They searched the Emergency Room and found numerous dead bodies, but they did not find Mrs. Gulledge. In the still air and extreme heat of the closed building, the odor of decaying bodies was horrible. Searching the morgue, they found more bodies, but still no Mrs. Gulledge. They noticed that in the morgue, the bodies had been stacked on top of each other, and they immediately returned to the Emergency Room for a more thorough search. Looking under every sheet and opening all of the plastic wrappings, they also discovered that bodies were stacked on top each other. There, they found Mrs. Gulledge. Senator Chaisson identified the body. The loss of a loved one is a painful experience. Having to identify a loved one under such extreme conditions had to have been a traumatic experience, which I am sure Senator Chaisson will carry for the rest of his life.

After securing the hospital door, they traveled back to St. Charles Parish. With this mission complete, the Chaisson family was allowed to have a proper burial for their grandmother the following Friday. Each of the officers involved in the search were listed as honorary pallbearers during the service.

Day Ten
Sunday, September 4, 2005

More Rescues in a Strange World

Following the St. Charles Emergency Operations Center's Saturday meeting, two National Guardsmen then assigned to St. Charles Parish advised that a military officer in Virginia had contacted them. The officer had heard of the successful Convention Center rescue operation conducted days before. As a favor, he asked if we would attempt to locate his niece at her French Quarter home and, if she was there, evacuate her. Normally, such a request would have been directed to the New Orleans Police Department. It is likely that the military officer didn't want to make a request to an overburdened police force. Much of the same team was assembled, only this time, Sheriff Greg Champagne came along.

When we arrived at the apartment, located on a narrow French Quarter street, the 150-year-old multiple family complex was secure, with no sign of activity inside. These historic structures actually face center courtyards, a private oasis sheltered from the busy traffic and constant noise of a part of the city that never sleeps.

One of the National Guardsmen climbed a large security gate and opened it from inside, allowing us access. On the second-floor apartment, we located a middle-aged lady, who seemed to be upset that her uncle had sent someone to evacuate her. Determined and defiant, she refused to leave, and asked if we could return in a few days, after she had had a chance to pack. Many of the team walked back to their police cars in disbelief, and the two Guardsmen were faced with a difficult decision. Should they force the lady to leave—an acceptable demand, since the entire city was under a mandatory evacuation order—or should they call a ranking military officer and explain why they had come back empty-handed?

After the better part of an hour, I convinced the woman that services would be out in the city for at least a month, and that if she wanted to return to her home to retrieve her belongings during the time the evacuation order was in effect, I would personally bring her to her home. She made me give her a business card with my cell number on it so she could contact me. With that, we all watched in amusement as the two Guardsmen carried boxes, bags, and dogs to their vehicle, until nothing else could fit. They returned back to St. Charles Parish while the rest of us continued on. We went to the First District Station, where Captain Walsdorf again met with his niece, while the rest of us went to the District Commander's office.

On our way, we noticed that vending machines barricaded the glass main doors to the station. Bullet holes in the glass and corresponding holes in the vending machines were evidence of the tense days and nights that preceded our visit. We sat and talked with New Orleans Police Captain Scott and Lieutenant Troy Savage. Many years earlier, Savage had been employed with the St. Charles Sheriff's Office. For over an hour, we listened attentively as they explained the never-ending challenges they faced. They spoke of the many rescues that

Chest Deep and Rising:

officers from that district had performed. Captain Scott also expressed the frustration of hearing voices calling for help, but not being able to find them. The sounds were apparently coming through vent pipes from people trapped in attics, sounds that were reflected through the still air and deafening silence of the flooded city in such a way that they sometimes couldn't locate the person before the cries for help faded.

Walking out of the lobby and into the parking garage, we saw a medic working out of the trunk of her car, a line of officers standing by her. One by one, she vaccinated officers with tetanus and hepatitis shots. I waited in line and took two of the three shots offered. Noticing she was running low on one of the two required hepatitis vaccinations, I told her to save it for a New Orleans Police officer.

As we left the station, I couldn't help wondering why the national media was so focused on everything that had gone wrong during the Hurricane Katrina response. Here were the real heroes: the officers down in the trenches. Most of them had lost their homes, some had lost family members, and all had loved ones evacuated to unknown cities, yet they remained on the job, rescuing their neighbors, protecting their city.

Down in "Da Parish"

After several failed attempts in the preceding days due to high floodwater, we all headed towards New Orleans East and then successfully into St. Bernard Parish, or, as locals affectionately call it, "Da Parish." Traveling on the elevated portions of Interstate 10, the large letter "H" could be seen painted on the roadway in several locations where landing zones for rescue helicopters were designated. Abandoned campsites, abandoned cars, and piles of trash were all along the roadway where many had been trapped for days. Where the elevated roadway met the ground level, we drove through water so deep that it poured through my police car's doors. It was too late to turn my police car around, so we forged ahead.

As we crossed the Interstate 10 "High Rise," a portion of Interstate 10 that crosses above the Industrial Canal, which, through a series of locks, links the Mississippi River, Lake Pontchartrain, and the Mississippi Gulf Outlet, the enormity of the flood was never more evident. From this vantage point, floodwaters were visible as far as the eye could see. A large ocean-going tug could be seen partially submerged; tugboats, large dry docks, and barges were on dry ground. They had been left there as the tidal surge allowed the vessels to float outside the canal before the water receded.

Traveling down Paris Road, an area where fishing marinas are prevalent, we saw boats and vehicles covering the roadway. A hotel used by traveling anglers had been destroyed, as had several other businesses in the area. It was as if the bottom eight feet of every building's walls had been ripped away, exposing the metal frames with the building's contents spewed out. As we entered St. Bernard Parish, we were in awe at the sheer destruction. Nothing had been spared. Every home and building in a parish with a population of 65,000 had flooded, to depths ranging from two to 15 feet. A watermark showing several feet of water inside the St. Bernard Parish Courthouse could be seen on the exterior walls, and several boats sat on the front lawn. They were still tied to trees, apparently used in rescue efforts before the water receded. Many areas were still flooded, making it difficult to maneuver anywhere other than the highest roadways. Not far away, the 911 Communication

Center was abandoned and in ruins, since it had gone completely underwater.

We stopped to talk to St. Bernard deputies who were working a traffic checkpoint. They explained that when Hurricane Katrina's winds started to diminish, the floodwaters started to rise rapidly. Using boats and Jet Skis, they rescued hundreds of residents from rooftops and brought them to higher ground. They also talked of the horrific find at St. Rita's Nursing Home, a senior home that failed to evacuate prior to the storm. Thirty-five people had drowned in the rapid rising floodwaters, one of whom, Emile Poissenot, 89, was a retired New Orleans Police officer.

After dropping off the remaining supplies, we made a list of the sheriff's deputies' personal needs, one of which was a desperate plea for one pound of fresh ground coffee. I promised to return the following day with new supplies. We headed back to St. Charles Parish, driving through the same floodwaters as we drove west on the eastbound lanes of Interstate 10. Driving alongside large high-rise buildings in darkness broken only by the strobe light on my police car gave an uneasy feeling.

Arriving at Destrehan High School, we found that volunteers had arrived in large numbers. The parking lot had filled quickly with police vehicles from various states. The gyms were teeming with activity. Many volunteers were already on shifts; those just arriving were anxious to go out. Needing to balance the shifts and with a greater need for day assignments, the volunteers were encouraged to get some rest after their long drives. It was apparent that many thought they were coming to rescue people from rooftops and arrest looters, tasks for which the need was rapidly diminishing. I knew it would be a matter of time before some would be disappointed with the less exciting yet necessary assignments that are required during disaster recovery efforts.

Arriving at my home, my household had grown by four. Gail's daughter, Denise, her husband, Tim, and their boys, Rhett and Ruston, had returned from an evacuation shelter in Grenada, Mississippi. Their home in Chalmette, Louisiana, had been destroyed. We sat and talked for hours about their ordeal. On the Friday before the storm, they had been excitedly anticipating a fishing trip near Delacroix Island in St. Bernard Parish, a place to which they had made many fishing trips. They had no idea that Hurricane Katrina's path had changed. When they woke Saturday morning and walked outside, it was apparent that the winds had changed. Turning on the Weather Channel, they learned of Hurricane Katrina's new path. The fishing trip was off! Having stayed at their home for other hurricanes, they gathered hurricane supplies and planned to do so again.

But by Sunday morning, St. Bernard Parish officials were broadcasting urgent appeals to residents to evacuate; family members were also frantic that they had not yet left. They boarded up their home, loaded two vehicles with the necessary items to last a couple days, and placed their two golden retrievers in one of the vehicles. Denise explained how she repeatedly sent her sons back into the house to return things they were trying to put in the car, insisting they would be home before they knew it.

Besides leaving possessions behind, they also left neighbors who refused to evacuate. Most figured they could deal with a power outage for a few days. One family that stayed behind was that of their sons' best friend. They waved to him from the back window of the car after pleading with him to talk his family into leaving. As they sat in endless lines of traf-

Chest Deep and Rising:

fic heading north, they realized that they had left too late: finding a hotel room was not going to be an easy task. After driving nearly 17 hours, they ended up in a Grenada, Mississippi, gas station parking lot at 4:00 in the morning, with no place to go.

A Grenada Police officer drove up and offered to take them to a church shelter. The officer had already rounded up several other carloads of stranded evacuees. A line of cars followed him to Emanuel Baptist Church. Along with 200 other evacuees, they spent the next seven days at the church. They were fed, given clothes, information, medical attention, and understanding. Even the dogs were treated well; a local veterinarian housed the dogs free of charge. Soon the group of bedraggled evacuees had become like family. The church organized activities for the children (movies, games, sports). Local organizations staged a barbecue, a fish fry, and a trip to the local high school football game. Brother Brad White organized the shelter for the church; he had done this before for other hurricanes and was well prepared. Denise commented to us that it was comforting to know that there were people in our world who spent their time and money helping complete strangers. Never in her life had she experienced such sheer generosity.

Although the church members, including the youth, worked hard to distract the evacuees, many were glued to the television, desperate for any news. Most of the news was about the Superdome and Convention Center. They wondered what had happened to their community, St. Bernard Parish. No news was forthcoming for a few days. Because of the crippled communication system, they couldn't contact family members or friends. Since they had never evacuated before when storms threatened, they knew family and friends would be worried about them after hearing the reports of death and destruction in St. Bernard Parish.

News began to trickle in about the flooding of St. Bernard Parish. Even though they had been told that every home in St. Bernard Parish was flooded, they did not believe it. The home they lived in had not flooded even during Hurricane Betsy. This was the hope they clung to for a few days. Denise's sons, Rhett and Ruston, grew increasingly worried about the friends who had stayed home. When news of the severe flooding came out, their parents assured them that their friends would surely have sought shelter at Chalmette High School. They soon heard, however, that the roof of Chalmette High School had collapsed, with 3,500 people inside the building.

After seven days at the shelter and with extra containers of gasoline for the trip, Denise and her family headed to my home in Norco. The disastrous effects of the storm became clearer and clearer the closer they got to St. Charles Parish. Soldiers and police officers were everywhere. Exits and entrances to the Interstate were blocked. Late that evening, they made it to my home. It would become their home as well for nine months.

Day Eleven
Monday, September 5, 2005

Help Begins to Arrive

Driving into the Destrehan High School parking lot on Monday, September 5th, I saw there was a great deal of activity. I noticed that United States Mint Police Inspector Lou Cannon, the Washington, DC, Fraternal Order of Police President, had arrived. He and the 27 United States Mint Police officers were unloading relief supplies that they had brought to assist in the recovery efforts. Bottled water, MREs, ammunition, personal hygiene products, disposal baby diapers, and the like—they had completely filled their vehicles. They brought with them anything and everything they thought would be of use. A special UPS delivery arrived as well—a large mobile kitchen, capable of turning out a high volume of meals daily. This kitchen is owned by a partnership with the Washington, DC, Fraternal Order of Police Labor Council and the Metropolitan Police Department. It is normally used to feed law enforcement officers during large security events in the nation's capital. Learning of our request to use the kitchen, UPS wasted no time in volunteering to tow the trailer to St. Charles Parish.

A good friend for many years, Inspector Cannon had driven all night and day and was exhausted, yet he couldn't sleep. Only able to stay one day before reporting back to Washington, DC, his visit had a dual purpose. He and his crew has been dispatched with the authority of the Secretary of the Treasury to assess the financial infrastructure in the affected region, and he wanted to personally make sure his officers and the mobile kitchen were in place and assisting in the recovery efforts. He explained that driving out of Alabama into Mississippi as he traveled south on Interstate 59, he had seen how the storm's destruction intensified with every mile they traveled. Having witnessed many natural disasters, he seemed to be taken aback by the enormity of the area of devastation and the level of damage, which covered three states and extended 120 miles, inland.

The kitchen was moved to an area between the gyms and a large classroom building. A school board electrician arrived and connected the power. Lighting the stove pilot light offered some entertainment for those seated on the picnic tables in front of the gym. St. Charles Sheriff's Office Sergeant Clyde Taylor and two trustees assigned to assist in setting up the police shelter were inside the kitchen, attempting to light the pilot light. Upon turning on the propane valve and then lighting a match, a small explosion rocked the mobile kitchen, the sound of which was apparently much worse than the flame itself. Nonetheless, one by one, the three of them were airborne as they exited the trailer, jumping further than Olympic gold medalists. A gas line had apparently ruptured during the 1,100-mile journey from Washington, DC. The story would be told and retold many times over. Each time, the distance they jumped grew further.

I was able to make contact with Johnny Frederic on the cell phone. With their truck filled with supplies, Johnny,

Tommy Tizzard, and Steve Juneau agreed to meet us in the Destrehan High School parking lot at 10:00 A.M. From there, we would travel to New Orleans and St. Bernard Parish with supplies, as promised the night before. Inspector Cannon and I made a quick pass by the St. Charles Emergency Operations Center in Hahnville. There, we received an update of the day's many challenges, but with the extra law enforcement personnel on site, things had begun to stabilize. After introducing Inspector Cannon to some of the parish officials at the Courthouse, we headed back to Destrehan High School and made plans to deliver the supplies brought by the Washington, DC, Fraternal Order of Police.

When we returned to Destrehan High School, Lenny Whetsel, a Senior Officer Specialist for the Federal Bureau of Prisons, was up and about. He had driven in from New Jersey the day before. He was drinking a cup of coffee with Lieutenant Wayne Lee, who was explaining the events of the previous days. I asked Lenny to join us for a run into New Orleans and St. Bernard Parish. Heavily armed and with vehicles loaded with supplies, we headed toward St. Bernard Parish. With a few requests for supplies in New Orleans, we planned stops on the way.

Once in the city, we passed by the Convention Center. With everyone evacuated, the building and surrounding area were in ruins. There was trash everywhere, and horrific smells. Chairs from nearby Mulate's restaurant and from the Convention Center were all over the place. For many in the group, this was the first sight of the city since they had attended the National Fraternal Order of Police Conference in this same building only four weeks earlier. They all seemed in awe as they pointed out locations and activities they had visited only weeks before.

Again, we stopped at Harrah's Casino, where the New Orleans Police had set up a command post. This time we were able to learn the location of a couple more districts. The increase in emergency personnel was blatantly obvious. Police cars and fire trucks, representing agencies from all across the United States, patrolled the streets. Also, National Guardsmen on foot patrol and security posts and in equipment convoys were throughout the city. At the water's edge, Search and Rescue teams boarded boats and began the grim task of searching every home for bodies.

From there, we proceeded to St. Bernard Parish. Once we entered Chalmette, an unincorporated town in St. Bernard Parish, it was horrible. Only hours before, I had traveled many of these same streets at sunset, but I was now seeing things I had not noticed the day before. There was so much wind and water damage. All was compounded by the smell of rotting vegetation from saltwater intrusion. It was all just unbelievable!

You could watch the television news coverage all day, but until you actually breathed the air, smelled the smells and walked the streets, you just can't understand the magnitude of the devastation. It is too much for the mind to comprehend. Strip malls, convenience stores, and restaurants: all had been completely destroyed by the forces of rushing water that pushed in the glass and brick fronts of buildings and washed everything inside the building right out the back. We passed by Chalmette High School and found extensive flood damage, but the roof was intact. There were no deaths reported at Chalmette High School. The reports Rhett and Ruston had heard on television while in the evacuation shelter in Grenada, Mississippi, were false. After days of worrying, the boys were relieved to learn this was just a rumor—one rumor among the many generated during and after the storm.

I found myself looking often at the expression on Inspector Cannon's face as we traversed the flooded cars and boats lining the roadway. For days, I had seen so much destruction; it was sort of like the officers at the First District who for hours explained their experiences. It was as if I had found comfort in having someone else see and understand what we had been dealing with for over a week.

The group decided to split up: some went with Lieutenant Lee, who wanted to inspect the damage to his home and two other family homes in different parts of Chalmette. The others continued on to deliver supplies. Traveling through more deep water as we passed patrol vehicles submerged underwater, we finally made it to the Port of St. Bernard where the St. Bernard Parish Sheriff's Office had established a supply depot. A sign identified the warehouse as "Camp Katrina." There, the parking lots were filled with their newly acquired police vehicles, a collection of the few vehicles in St. Bernard Parish that had not flooded. They were mostly pick-up trucks. The letters "SBSO" or "POLICE" had been spray-painted freehand on the vehicle's doors to identify their authority.

As we approached the entrance of the warehouse, we were stopped to allow two helicopters to land. Several people greeted the passengers and escorted them to the warehouse, where a crowd was gathered. Everything was at a standstill. Concerned that I would not be able to unload the supplies and still have enough time to assess the damage to Denise's home before nightfall, we backed the trailer up to the front corner of the warehouse and started unloading the supplies. It was then we learned what the excitement was about. Superstar actor John Travolta and his actress wife Kelly Preston had flown in to lift the spirits of the isolated St. Bernard Parish deputies, and from the looks of it, they had done a good job. My first thoughts were that we had too much work to do during a crisis without catering to movie stars. My opinion quickly changed, however. Excited Hurricane Katrina survivors flocked around them, taking photographs, getting autographs, sharing their storm experiences with the very attentive movie stars. For each of the newly homeless, this was one of the few possessions they now owned. Travolta and Preston's brief trip was a tremendous morale boost for a region that had not only been devastated, but also isolated from the rest of the world for over a week. Their visit showed these Hurricane Katrina victims they had not been forgotten.

Traversing the streets of Chalmette in an attempt to locate Denise's home on Corinne Drive had gotten complicated. Covering a large area of Chalmette was a thick layer of crude oil. The thick, black oil coated everything: homes, cars, boats, trees, and pets. We eventually made it to Denise's home, but with the windows boarded, it was difficult to accurately assess the damage. The exterior suggested that they had had about five feet of water in their home, but the water had already receded. Lieutenant Lee met us, and we learned that his home had experienced the same level of water, ruining everything inside.

From there, we proceeded to Lower St. Bernard Parish, to the family home of National Guard Sergeant Bier. It was a wood-framed house elevated off the ground on pillars and on high land; we were unable to enter the residence to determine the extent of damage, but it appeared minimal. However, a vintage car and farm tractor parked in the garage both appeared to have been flooded.

As we passed through subdivisions, we saw packs of dogs roaming the streets. From shepherds to poodles, and all breeds in between, they instinctively banded together in search of food. Once, we stopped to check a home and were startled when a pack of 20 or so dogs rushed towards us. They were covered in sludge and oil, but clearly they were someone's pets. Residents had been forced to leave their pets behind, since most evacuation shelters would not allow them. Having been on their own for nearly two weeks, their ragged tails wagged as they approached us in search of food. Nonetheless, when that many animals rush toward you, it is intimidating. My first reaction was to shout at the pack, causing them to slow their movement. From that point on, many of the officers would bring bags of dog food and spill it on street corners to feed these forgotten Hurricane Katrina victims.

During the dark, eerie ride back to St. Charles Parish, Lenny Whetsel commented that it reminded him of a horror movie, depicting the aftermath of a nuclear bomb, with you the only one still alive. Traffic lights were not working, there were no lights, and nothing was moving; just a screen door flapping in the wind. Crossing the Mississippi River Gulf Outlet Bridge, we could see the New Orleans skyline from the moonlight, but there weren't any lights on in the city. If you didn't know the city was there, you probably wouldn't have noticed it.

We returned to Destrehan High School, not a moment too soon. Two days without sleep had caught up with Inspector Cannon, and he needed to get an early start in the morning for a drive back to Washington, DC, where he would help coordinate the infusion of money into the local economy to help support a market once dependent on electronic transactions.

With plans to deliver more relief supplies the next morning, Johnny went back to Baton Rouge to reload with provisions that members of the Baton Rouge Lodge had assisted in acquiring. I headed home to show Denise and Tim the photos I had taken of their destroyed home, and Lenny

Whetsel met up with Detective Ganote and Detective Sergeant Renee Kinler to work night patrol and answer calls for a while before calling it a night.

Day Twelve
Tuesday, September 6, 2005

Angola South

Waiting for me on the island counter in the kitchen of my home on Tuesday morning was a note, a short list of items, and a house key. Denise asked if, when I returned to Chalmette, I could pass by her home and collect a few items. With plans to return and deliver supplies that day, I promised I would try to retrieve the items.

While traveling to Destrehan High School, I received a message from Johnny Frederic to call New Orleans Police Lieutenant Julie Wilson. She identified the terrible conditions in which she and her officers were living. Lieutenant Wilson had heard from other officers that the Fraternal Order of Police was delivering supplies, and asked if we could help out her district as well. Although the Fifth District had set up in the lobby of the New Orleans Sheraton Hotel, they were in need of personal hygiene supplies, fresh underwear, clothing, and cell phone chargers and batteries. She gave me a list of supplies and asked that I contact her when I reached New Orleans.

Arriving at the school, I asked Susie Breaux and Lori Duplessis to go to the Special Services Building in Hahnville to retrieve all the chargers and batteries they could from cell phones donated to a program where discarded cell phones are programmed to dial 911 and given to people with special needs. Johnny Frederic and Pete Burque arrived with a truckload of supplies and police shirts. However, with the added supplies that had to be delivered, we needed more cargo space. Lenny Whetsel brought with him something that would prove to be of great value in the recovery effort. Scott G. Wampler Lodge #148, Fraternal Order of Police, from New Jersey, of which Lenny is the Lodge President, had a box trailer that was the perfect size for maneuvering in and out of the affected areas on our daily supply runs. I asked Lenny if we could use the trailer, and before I could finish explaining why, he started removing his personal equipment to make room for the relief supplies.

Our first stop was at a local warehouse where supplies were being stored. We loaded the trailer and the back of his truck with everything in the warehouse. While we were at the warehouse, Special Agent Anneva DeConto, with Immigrations and Customs Enforcement and a member of the Washington, DC, Fraternal Order of Police, called and said that Galls, a national police supplier, and their parent company, Aramark, were sending a tractor trailer loaded with BDU uniforms, hygiene items and medical items, and other supplies, with a promise they would be delivered to Destrehan High School the following day. This was a welcome message, as uniforms seemed to be in great need, but were the hardest to come by.

We decided to take a different route into the city that day. With floodwaters receding, we traveled on the east bank towards the Interstate 10 and Causeway Blvd overpass, an area used as a triage and staging area for evacuations. I had heard stories from other officers who had passed there. Their descriptions were very accurate. There, the normally busy interchange was disgusting, to say the least. The few people still there were standing in lines and they were ankle deep in slop. The smell left no doubt—it was a mixture of rainwater and bodily fluids. From there, we headed to the River Road. Along the Mississippi River, land is higher, allowing us to bypass floodwaters and gain access to the City of New Orleans. Our first stop was Harrah's Casino. This time, we were able to find the location of other temporary districts.

We proceeded to the Union Passenger Terminal on Loyola Avenue, an area near where the flooding begins. There, we met with Major Roland Ladreyt, a member of my department detailed to the Louisiana Attorney General's Office. Major Ladreyt gave us a tour of what had become New Orleans' newest jail. The region now had a place to put looters who were arrested. However, the location of this seriously needed facility had been discovered purely by chance.

Major Ladreyt explained how Burl Cain, warden of the Louisiana State Penitentiary better known as Angola, and several of his officers came across the Union Passenger Terminal, a facility that serves both as an Amtrak train station and a Greyhound bus station. The building was being looted. As they pulled into the parking lot, the looters scattered in different directions. They were trying to break into a safe and steal gifts from the terminal gift shop, and helping themselves to anything and everything that wasn't bolted down. Walking through the abandoned building, it struck Warden Cain that the area would be suitable for a temporary jail. It hadn't flooded. There was easy access to the elevated Interstate 10 and Crescent City Connection Bridge. Both roadways were the lifelines in and out of New Orleans.

Major Ladreyt explained how Richard L. Stalder, Secretary of the Louisiana Department of Public Safety and Corrections and Charles Foti, a longtime sheriff of Orleans Parish before being elected Louisiana Attorney General, had helped set up the makeshift jail. In the lobby and under bus awnings outside, kennel-type cages were constructed, into which arrestees were placed before being transported to other, more permanent, correctional facilities. They initially called the facility Camp Greyhound, then Camp Amtrak, both as a way of expressing appreciation to those entities for allowing the jail in their building, to remain on site, and for all the assistance they rendered in keeping the facility open. It was later decided that it might not be a good idea to have these corporate names associated with a jail. With that, the name was changed to Angola South.

Saying the passenger terminal was a jail did not give justice to the function it served, or the efforts it took operate it. The facility required quick and creative thinking, and was perhaps the single biggest action in bringing law and order back to the region. A mini-justice system had to be created from the ground up, and all within the same building. Amtrak locomotives were used to provide electrical power to the entire complex. A complex judicial support system needed to be created. Arrestees had to be properly identified, receive immediate medical treatment and assessment, fingerprinted, their valuable property collected, bonds set, arraignment, and release procedures set up. A system had to be created to track every arrest and charge. Arrest reports had to be filed and evidence collected on site.

The makeshift jail served multiple law enforcement agencies trying to effect arrests in different jurisdictions. Many were not familiar with the New Orleans police reports, and out-of-state officers were not familiar with state statutes and violations. From a hurricane-ravaged and looted Wal-Mart, Major Ladreyt acquired locks, used to secure lockers where evidence was to be stored. Also established was an area for the New Orleans District Attorney to review police reports and keep copies of all arrests. Additionally, an area was set up for the U.S. Attorney's office, which also reviewed each arrest for possible federal charges.

For communications, they wired telephones in the building to a portable satellite system that rerouted calls out of state and then back into the area. The facility was not used exclusively by New Orleans; they received and processed all arrests from Plaquemines, Jefferson, and St. Bernard Parishes, since Hurricane Katrina had disabled all jails in these four parishes. In some cases, these parishes had no judicial system intact; no judge to set bonds.

During the days that immediately followed the storm, bullet holes in the glass and building walls impressed upon each officer the need to wear protective gear. Eventually they were able to light up the surrounding area, establishing a more secure perimeter and making the area much safer.

Within an hour of his first day at the jail, someone reported to Major Ladreyt that they had seen a woman waving something out of a 23rd floor window of an office building across the street from Angola South. The 30-story building was being renovated, with asbestos remediation placards posted all around the building. Looters had broken into this and all surrounding buildings and pillaged anything of value they could find.

With evidence that the building had been broken into and no way to confirm the reports of a woman calling for help from a window where curtains could be seen blowing in the wind, a seven-man entry team with the Louisiana Attorney Generals Task Force entered the building and conducted a floor-to-floor search.

Concerned there might be armed looters inside the building, they carefully searched each floor, in full riot gear in the sweltering heat, as they ascended to the 23rd floor. Soaked in sweat from the heavy gear, their anxiety grew each time they passed a placard labeled "warning: asbestos contamination." Judging from the damage, empty beer and liquor bottles, looters had had free run of the building. Fortunately, they found the building to be unoccupied.

Major Ladreyt spoke of his experiences just a few days earlier, visiting the New Orleans Police Department Fourth District on the west bank. Although the area did not flood, Hurricane Katrina's ferocious winds had destroyed the building. Case files, including unsolved murder cases, were exposed to anyone wanting to enter the building. A lone officer watched over the building, trying to keep the area secure. The remainder of the Fourth District officers had regrouped in the back of a Wal-Mart store. A couple of days later, after establishing a line of communication with the Fourth District commanders, Major Ladreyt was able to get a large generator to light up the area outside the building in order to maintain security at night.

With the flooded Orleans Parish Prison evacuated and shut down, two Orleans Parish Criminal Sheriff's Office deputies, who had swum out of the facility and participated in the original prison evacuation, reported to Angola South. They had nowhere else to go and were looking for assignments. Both had prior military experience and, along with Major Ladreyt, worked both inside the makeshift jail and on foot patrols along the parameter.

Chest Deep and Rising:

One of the deputies commented that the night missions reminded him of his recon foot patrols in abandoned, bombed-out areas of cities in Bosnia, looking for snipers. With a single pair of night vision goggles they searched for looters, snipers and, in particular, an arsonist who was repeatedly setting buildings ablaze at night. With the ability to fight fires seriously hampered due to a lack of water pressure and equipment destroyed by flooding, this was cause for tremendous concern. Although they did not catch the arsonist, they eventually made an arrest of a person they suspected. With that arrest, the nighttime fires ceased.

The Forgotten American Flag

We met Lieutenant Wilson, whom we followed to the Sheraton Hotel on Canal Street, the new Fifth District. In sweltering heat and humidity, several officers slept on cots in the noisy and very busy lobby. The place was abuzz with activity, officers walking in and out, hotel maintenance crews working tirelessly to reestablish power and water pressure in an effort to restart the hotel. In one reception salon, a room full of people recovered financial records and other electronic data from the hotel's computer system. These officers must have been exhausted to be able to sleep with that much activity going on around them.

The Sheraton is located on the world-renowned Canal Street, the westward dividing line between the French Quarter and the Business District. On the Canal Street median, only 11 days earlier, electric streetcars powered by overhead cables had systematically carried passengers from the River Front and the St. Charles Avenue Lines. Now, the median was covered with motor coaches, television production trucks with large satellite dishes pointed skyward, bright lights, and generators. The spectacle stretched 20 city blocks and represented every news agency in the free world. We coined it the "Media Circus," as at any given time, there appeared to be three or more shows underway on each block.

Talking with officers in the Sheraton, we discovered another very useful service the Fraternal Order of Police could provide. Communications were still hit-and-miss, with much of the communications infrastructure in disarray. Several officers gave us names and numbers to call to let people know they were okay. This was the beginning of a messaging service run through the Louisiana Fraternal Order of Police Office in Baton Rouge. Each day's delivery usually included message relays.

After unloading supplies and making a list of additional needs at the Fifth District, we drove down Bourbon Street into the French Quarter. It looked as if someone had overturned several dumpsters. Trash and debris still covered the streets, but there was no flooding. Following a brief stop at the First District, we split up. Johnny Frederic and his gang would make deliveries to the other New Orleans Police districts that we were able to identify, after which he would return to Baton Rouge to purchase a trailer similar to the one Lenny Whetsel had provided from New Jersey.

Lenny Whetsel, Deputy Charles Cardella from Ouahita Parish Sheriff's Office and myself went back to St. Bernard Parish to drop off supplies. All along Chef Menteur Boulevard in New Orleans East, crews working in recovery teams were using boats to search flooded neighborhoods by going house to house. After searching each home, a large X was spray painted on the residence, with notations listed in each of the quadrants. The top left identified the team searching, the top right listed the date, the bottom left identified the number of bodies discovered, and the bottom right was left open, but would later be used by animal rescue groups to identify the recovery of pets.

As we arrived at Denise's home in Chalmette, we noticed that the water damage on the exterior was much more noticeable in the daylight. Unlocking the door would prove to be challenging. Saltwater inside the locking mechanism had caused the moving parts to corrode and rust. When we entered the house, the intrusiveness of floodwaters was overwhelming. With the house completely sealed for over a week in intense heat, black mold was everywhere, and two inches of wet sludge covered the floor and walls. The rising and settling water levels had "rearranged" the furniture. It was as if everything were in black and white: the sludge had deposited a grayish tint on everything below the waterline. The only color came from a vivid green chevalier plant lying precariously among the rearranged living room furniture. The greenhouse-like temperature and humidity inside the closed home allowed the plant to thrive. The water was so intrusive, I wondered if a single thing below the waterline could be salvaged.

Going through the list, I slowly collected the items Denise wanted and carried them to the trailer outside. Baseball trophies, sports memorabilia, academic awards, autographed baseballs, and engraved bats from the boys' rooms; a couple of boxes from the attic; and from the master bedroom, paperwork from atop a dresser and multiple boxes of 35mm slides that told their family story in pictures. Behind the boxes in the closet, I discovered one item not on the list, but something that would make the trip home with us—a folded American flag. We loaded the items into the trailer and headed home.

We arrived at my house. Denise and her family met us in the driveway. As Lenny Whetsel opened the trailer, I tried to prepare them so they would not have unrealistic expectations of what was salvageable. One by one, we pulled the items out of the trailer and their eyes lit up. The boys went through their trophies and medals; Tim grabbed the boxes of slides and began to inspect them. Stored above the waterline, they had been recovered before the moisture ruined them. I think that as long as we all live, we will never forget the emotions displayed when I handed them the American flag. It had been draped on the coffin of Tim's father, a World War II veteran. Concealed behind boxes, they had forgotten it was in the closet. Although they had lost their home, they had something from their past to hold onto. Many of Hurricane Katrina's victims would be deprived such a courtesy. Some Hurricane Katrina victims would be unable to even find their homes.

Day Thirteen
Wednesday, September 7, 2005

800 Crutches

We woke the next morning to the sight of a fully loaded tractor-trailer of equipment from Galls and Aramark. We knew it had to be unloaded, but with no forklift, about 20 officers would have to do the job manually. The main cargo we needed was the BDU uniforms, but getting to them would not be an easy task. The BDU uniforms were loaded at the front of the trailer, and tons of other supplies would have to be unloaded first: since the boxes of uniforms took up only about one-third of the trailer space, the Atlanta, Georgia trucking company that transported the supplies proceeded to load the remaining portions of the trailer with surplus supplies from around their warehouse—bandages; large, military-grade water bladders; suntan lotion; plates; gloves; and even about 800 pairs of wooden crutches. I jokingly suggested that they had heard Hurricane Katrina had crippled Louisiana, so they sent us crutches. From Deputy Chief to academy recruits and every rank in between, all pitched in as we formed an assembly line to unload the truck. This was time-consuming and exhausting, but it was done.

I made contact with Keith McCrary, the Mississippi Fraternal Order of Police State President, since he represented an area that in many cases was even more devastated than Louisiana. They, too, had established supply lines to not only the Gulf Coast, but to the many towns and cities that were devastated by tornadoes as Hurricane Katrina traveled inland, deep into Mississippi.

Displaced from his severely damaged home, Mississippi State Lodge Secretary Wilber Chamberlin and other Fraternal Order of Police members began a delivery operation of tens of thousands of dollars' worth of food, water, clothing, and police supplies to police departments along the Mississippi Gulf Coast and well inland. The communities of Bay St. Louis, Pass Christian, Gautier, Biloxi, Gulfport, Long Beach and Waveland experienced such widespread destruction that some communities were completely washed away by the violent storm surge. Chamberlin wasn't working alone; during this time he had the full support of his family, including his son, ten-year-old Jordan, who was by his side, helping load and unload vehicles and making several trips with him to the Gulf Coast. A team of Mint Police Officers were routed to Mississippi to meet up with Wilber to share the supplies we had received from Galls and the "POLICE" shirts we had made.

With the trucks and trailers loaded, the daily deliveries to the various districts began. Lieutenant Pam Negrotto and I rode in Lenny Whetsel's truck. We delivered supplies to the New Orleans Police Department, Jefferson Parish Sheriff's Office and Plaquemines Sheriff's Office, and the New Orleans Harbor Police.

As we were preparing to leave for New Orleans, Chief Cardella asked us to deliver supplies to New Orleans Police Captain Timmy Bayard, a narcotics commander leading water rescue effort in the City of New Orleans. The Chief had met with him the day before, and relayed the many heroic rescues Captain Bayard and his officers had undertaken. With no working radios, Captain Bayard's small team began to realize that thousands of people had been trapped in their homes and businesses. He immediately organized and coordinated the rescue of as many people as possible. He did not, initially, have the resources needed. With boats supplied by individual police officers under his command, rescue efforts commenced as soon as they could place a boat in the water.

He, along with his rescuing heroes, sustained a daily grind from sunrise to sunset, plucking thousands of people from rooftops and bringing them to higher ground. In the initial days of the rescue efforts, Captain Bayard had to order his officers to cease their rescue efforts at darkness, due to the lack of proper lighting equipment for their rescue craft. Floating debris, down power lines, partially submerged objects, made it too dangerous and jeopardized the safety of not only the officers, but those they were attempting to rescue.

At nightfall, they experienced the personal horrors of knowing that thousands who were still stranded would have to try and survive another night without food or water. Captain Bayard sympathized with his officers when they had to be ordered to return to the launching dock. He was fully aware that many instances of gunfire were not of a violent nature, but rather that of an alert by stranded individuals. Floating around these once familiar neighborhoods, but now at a rooftop level, the officers had difficulty pinpointing the location or source of the alert gunfire.

Chief Cardella went on to say that the narcotics division had set up a temporary station in the English Turn

Subdivision on the west bank of New Orleans and I promised we would make a pass there to drop off supplies.

With National Guard deployment taking shape and with the majority of the city being evacuated, the New Orleans Police Department started offering their exhausted officers a chance to reunite with their families and make housing arrangements. At the discretion of district commanders, officers were allowed to rotate on five-day furloughs. Before taking leave, however, they were sent to the Belmont Hotel in Baton Rouge for triage and debriefing. In the hotel ballroom was a dormitory setting, FEMA representatives available to answer questions, and medical personnel and psychologists. Since the Belmont was only about two miles from the Baton Rouge Lodge home, Jim Gallagher printed flyers and began going to the Belmont daily to let officers know where to locate the Baton Rouge Fraternal Order of Police Shelter and the services offered.

Beginning our delivery route, our first stop was the New Orleans Police Department's First District Station. Captain Jimmy Scott was having a meeting with his officers. He thanked them for holding the city together during such a difficult time. He explained details of the furlough and the need to pass through the Belmont Hotel in Baton Rouge for debriefing before going on leave. He asked for volunteers for the first round of leave, but also asked the officers to consider their brother and sister officers and allow those with exceptional needs to go first. He did not say so, but some clearly needed leave to maintain their sanity, and he knew it. He explained the challenges of traveling out of the city and the high price of gasoline. The good news, he explained, was that the department would be issuing paychecks, including their overtime, something that would prove to be problematic for the City's finances and had caused a delay in payment for many frustrating days. With credit cards and ATMs out of service, furloughed officers had leave, but no cash.

Ft. Wal-Mart

We proceeded to a Wal-Mart Store on Tchopitoulas Street, perhaps one of the safest places in the City of New Orleans. Days earlier, the store had been ransacked by looters. Now it was being referred to as "Fort Wal-Mart," and it certainly resembled a fortified military encampment. It was the new command post for the officers of the Sixth District, an area covering portions of uptown and mid-city areas of New Orleans. As we arrived, we saw Captain Anthony Cannatella standing on a chair outside the building, with over 120 officers standing around him as he explained the furlough details. You could hear a pin drop; both Captain Cannatella and First District Captain Scott had clearly earned the respect of their officers.

Forced out of their station by flooding and wind damage, 120 police officers of the New Orleans Police Department's Sixth District now called this store their home, where they slept, worked, and lived in tents and cars in the store parking lot. Also assigned to the Sixth District, was 80-year-old Sergeant Manuel Curry, who has been a New Orleans Police officer since 1946. He joined the force after serving in WWII; he participated in D-Day, having landed at Omaha Beach in Normandy. A legend in Louisiana law enforcement, Sergeant Curry had "topped out" of his police pension over two decades earlier and was eligible to receive 100% of his salary upon retiring, yet he is still on the job, basically working for free. His life is the New Orleans Police Department, and his family and friends are those who wear a badge.

Understandably so, the officers in the Sixth District are quite protective of their mentor. Sergeant Curry had been ordered to leave to join his wife of 50 years, who had evacuated safely before the storm, but knowing she was safe with family members, he refused. Sergeant Curry said he had been with fellow officers throughout the storm and intended to stay with them as long as it took. Somehow, a stretch limousine had found its way to the Wal-Mart parking lot. Parked among police vehicles and tents erected in the parking lot, the limousine, a gift from the other officers, became the sleeping quarters for Sergeant Curry for several weeks.

While we were there, I spoke with Captain Tony Cannatella, a 3rd generation police officer who joined the ranks of the New Orleans Police Department in May of 1967. His father, his two brothers, his son, his nephew and his uncle are or were all police officers. A 38-year veteran of the New Orleans Police Department, Canatella had also "topped out" in his pension benefits years earlier and was also eligible for full pay upon retirement, yet remained on the job. It was easy to see why he was so respected by his officers. When asked how he was doing, with no hesitation, he smiled, and in a confident and commanding voice, he responded, "Where else can you work every single day and stand alongside real heroes?" He was right; the officers in his district, his department, and agencies all across the Gulf South were heroes. They had held it together during the region's darkest moments, and had truly made a difference.

At Fort Wal-Mart, the Sixth District Officers had coordinated water and rooftop rescue missions and looting patrols for days. Captain Cannatella supervised the establishment of a makeshift police station, dormitory, kitchen, dining area, first-aid station, food and water distribution center and a citizen evacuation site.

Although much of the Wal-Mart store had been looted before their arrival, Sixth District Officers were able to secure the store early enough to save needed supplies that would prove vital for the rescue efforts that followed. Captain Cannatella received permission to commandeer much of the items necessary for his, and other districts to function. His temporary police station quickly became the center for emergency relief supplies for police officers and other first responders operating in the now devastated city.

In preparation for Hurricane Katrina's arrival, Captain Cannatella had his entire fleet of police vehicles moved into a high-rise parking garage in his district. As winds reached 45mph, his entire compliment of officers reported to the 6th District Station, where they rode out the storm. In the immediate aftermath, Captain Cannatella directed members of his district to commandeer heavy construction equipment from a nearby work site and began clearing the streets of his district of downed trees, abandoned vehicles and storm debris to allow response to emergency calls.

Eventually, with floodwaters rising to unsafe levels, Captain Cannatella moved his entire staff to some of the highest ground in the city, the Wal-Mart parking lot. From that vantage point, the Sixth District officers began rescue operations. Captain Cannatella instructed several of his officers, who brought with them their personal watercraft, to begin rescue operations. During the days that immediately followed Hurricane Katrina's arrival, they were able to rescue hundreds of storm victims trapped in attics and on rooftops.

Early on, rather than leave looted items on the ground,

officers would collect and place them in one of two large trailers in the store parking lot for safekeeping. Speaking with other officers in the Sixth District, this reasonable practice eventually caused many officers much concern. News coverage of the Hurricane Katrina aftermath had become very critical of the New Orleans Police Department. They feared that television news cameras capturing them carrying these stolen goods would give the impression that they were participating in the looting as well.

Unloading boxes of uniforms and supplies and assessing their future needs, with a promise to bring additional supplies the following day, we moved on. We were able to make contact with Lieutenant Joe Labarriere of the New Orleans Harbor Police Department, and he met up with us at Ft. Wal-Mart. He and most of his department's 63 officers had ridden out the storm at the Hilton Riverside Hotel, at the foot of Canal Street next to the Mississippi River. He talked about watching the destruction through his 9th floor window, as the 29-story building swayed noticeably from side to side in the hurricane-force winds. Once the winds had subsided and the water began to rise, members of his department participated in hundreds of rescue operations in the Lower Ninth Ward area of the city.

Fats Domino

Lieutenant Labarriere spoke of one rescue in particular. Harbor Police Sergeant Steven Dorsey, Corporals Robert Lincoln and Glenn Smith, and Officer Christopher Lanier were rescuing residents in the rapidly flooding Lower Ninth Ward. Residents were stranded on the roofs of their homes. Dodging debris, partially submerged power lines and other hazards that made maneuvering a difficult task, they rescued hundreds of people from rooftops and brought them to the St. Claude Street Bridge, where they were then taken to the Louisiana Superdome. Around 10:00 P.M., their boat engines idling in total darkness as they drifted in the Lower Ninth Ward, they heard someone calling out for help on Caffin Avenue.

Carefully making their way to the two-story home, they were surprised to learn the cries for help were coming from the home of Antoine Domino, better known as "Fats Domino," Grammy winner and member of the Rock and Roll Hall of Fame, who had recorded hit songs in the 1950s and 1960s. The rescue boat pulled alongside a second-floor balcony, where Fats, his wife, and seven other relatives were rescued and taken to higher ground.

As were about one-third of his coworkers in the Harbor Police Department, Lieutenant Labarriere was homeless. Not because his home had been destroyed: he had received notice that his landlord intended to take advantage of the high demands for livable housing and sell the home while the market was inflated. The out-of-state owner asked Lieutenant Labarriere to vacate the home as soon as possible. Lieutenant Labarriere spoke with emotion as he explained that his wife and daughter had rented a house in Franklin, LA, a couple hours' drive from New Orleans, but they were okay and would be fine. Dropping off supplies at his station at the New Orleans Riverfront, we spoke to more officers who were dealing with the same housing and family issues.

As we drove through the city, evidence of the water level dropping was encouraging, but still demonstrated the difficulty of pumping the city dry. Miles away from the lowest part of New Orleans, it was painfully clear that access to much of the city would be many weeks away. We were, however, able to travel in areas that only days before, had had several feet of standing water. With downed trees and power lines still covering many roads, we wound through the city as if we were going through a maze.

At the New Orleans Police Department's triage and debriefing center, at the Belmont Hotel in Baton Rouge, Jim Gallagher learned two things. First, officers had no money and no way of getting any. ATMs and banks were still inoperative, and with a direct deposit payroll system in place before the storm, the city had not issued paychecks. Second, officers were reluctant to speak to psychologists about their ordeal. (Gallagher made contact with the chief psychologist at the Belmont and was granted permission to bring in peer counselors at the hotel.)

In addition, at the Baton Rouge Lodge, officers, whether members or not, could show their police credentials and were given gas stipends to reunite with their families, compliments of the Louisiana Fraternal Order of Police. Noticing that the gas stipend process was taking 15 or 20 minutes for each officer, at the first opportunity Gallagher grabbed Baton Rouge Lodge member Randy Watson to ask why he was putting officers through the wringer just to give them a few bucks for gas. To Gallagher's chagrin, Watson explained that the officers were themselves taking so much time. This, after all, was the first opportunity for many of them to speak to another law enforcement officer about their ordeals during the storm. Some were simply breaking down and crying, concerned about their families and future. From that point on, peer counselors became a regular part of the gas stipend process.

Never before had I received more hugs from men and women alike than when I gave them a package of underwear. Just imagine being in the same clothes for nine days, with your home, your possessions, and your police station destroyed. The uniforms were a welcome change, and officers lined up to find their size. In all, over 3,000 uniforms would be handed out over the next few days, to virtually every department in southeast Louisiana. You could tell that these officers were tired. Despite what the media was reporting, these officers were still on the job, still holding their own, and upholding the oath to protect and serve.

Also with us were Mike Haley, Terry Hofecker, and Sergeant Craig Hungler, all three part of the National Fraternal Order of Police Critical Incident Response Team. The three of them had spent months in New York, serving as law enforcement peer counselors following the September 11th attack on the World Trade Center. The Southern Law Enforcement Foundation, a Louisiana-based Critical Incident Peer Counselors Organization, operated out of the Louisiana Fraternal Order of Police office in Baton Rouge. They coordinated efforts statewide, and these three men made contact with officers at stops we made. When needed, one would stay at that district and talk with the police officers.

We later stopped at the New Orleans Steamship Company Wharf, where we met with New Orleans Police Lieutenant Henry Dean, president of the Crescent City Fraternal Order of Police, assigned to the traffic division, Dean and his officers had taken over the American Queen cruise terminal, at which passengers of the Delta Queen Steamboat Company board the luxury paddle wheeler for weeklong excursions up the Mississippi River. Inside the warehouse, they had set up a supply depot and a sleeping area.

I explained the number of services and recovery efforts being offered to the officers, and asked how he was making out. I asked how his home had fared and, with a grin on his face, he said he had eight inches of water. Making light of the situation, I suggested that wasn't bad. Lieutenant Dean laughed and said that the eight inches of water were all on the second floor. He went on to explain that his family had found a place to stay in Baton Rouge and were doing fine. His officers were all doing well; that was what was really important. He was right! Having seen the death and destruction that Hurricane Katrina brought to his city, it made it easier to truly understand how blessed he was and what was really important. After sharing some small talk, we dropped off supplies and moved on.

After nightfall, we attempted to locate Captain Bayard and his Vice Squad at English Turn. Officers throughout the region had learned a quick lesson in light discipline. With power out and the city in total darkness, lights attracted attention that wasn't always friendly. At other district stations in New Orleans, lights had attracted sniper fire. This resulted in spending the nights in darkness despite having the ability to get power from generators. We later learned we had actually passed within a block of them. With the power out and their makeshift station in total darkness, they were well hidden.

We decided to take the remaining supplies to Plaquemines Parish, located not far from where we where. There we met with Captain Chuck Adams with the Plaquemines Parish Sheriff's Office and dropped off the supplies in Belle Chasse and learned that almost the entire parish south of a community called Myrtle Grove was still under water, and was expected to be so for weeks. I spoke to Colonel Charles Guey by telephone. I offered him two large water bladders that had been delivered with the uniforms. The bladders would later be filled and flown by helicopter to different parts of lower Plaquemines Parish that were completely cut off from the mainland.

Late that night, we returned to St. Charles Parish. Dropping everyone off, I drove 40 miles west to Gonzales, where another officer met me and dropped off Retired Federal Bureau of Prisons, Lieutenant Gabe Kitka, a member of Lenny Whetsel's Fraternal Order of Police Lodge in New Jersey. With the New Orleans Airport still closed, Kitka had flown into Baton Rouge to help in the relief efforts. We met in the parking lot of the Tanger Outlet Mall, where there was a Wendy's Hamburger Restaurant drive-through window open near the entrance. That hot hamburger, eaten on a picnic bench in front of a closed IZOD Outlet Store, was one of the best meals I had ever eaten! After talking a little, we traveled back to St. Charles Parish, where I dropped Gabe off at Destrehan High School and called it a night.

As Lenny Whetsel showered that evening at Destrehan High School, he heard an officer complaining about being assigned to assist in crowd control duties at a Wal-Mart. Lenny reminded him that if he didn't work that assignment, a local officer would have to, and that would take away manpower from the local Sheriff's Office. Lenny reminded him that not all assignments were glamorous, and that this type of work is the reality of recovery from a disaster. The officer didn't have much more to say that night.

Day Fourteen
Thursday, September 8, 2005

Route to North Shore

The morning of Thursday, September 8th started with the same problem that Lenny Whetsel had dealt with the night before. One of the officers from a visiting agency did not like his assignment at a Wal-Mart store, where hundreds of people stood in long lines, hopeful for a chance to purchase much-needed supplies. He and his buddies had left their post for a sightseeing trip into New Orleans and, in doing so, had placed the safety of the public and other officers in danger. He told me that he had found an agency that said they could use his help, but did not have a place for him and his four coworkers to bunk at night. He wanted to know if they could work with the other agency and spend their nights at Destrehan High School.

Normally I wouldn't have had a problem with it; several law enforcement officers at our shelter were assigned to other parishes. But this one was different. The disgruntled officers had been given an assignment and abandoned their post without advising anyone they were leaving. Had a St. Charles deputy done the same, there would have been severe consequences. They, however, were volunteers. I told them I thought it would be best if they found a different shelter, and suggested they contact the Louisiana Sheriff's Association, which operated a shelter in Gonzales. I didn't want them telling others it was okay to abandon their post in search of a more exciting assignment.

I knew that most of the assignments I had to offer were thankless and boring, but in disaster recovery, this is the real work. The need for rescue is immediately after the storm; recovery, however, takes months, and the services we were providing were vital to the recovery efforts. Recognizing that each officer needed a chance to see what was going on in other areas, we started to rotate both visiting officers and St. Charles deputies on the supply runs each day.

With the region showing signs of stabilizing, we decided to work a little smarter and divide up into different regions and delivery routes. Lieutenant George Breedy joined Lenny Whetsel and Gabe Kitka in deliveries to the New Orleans Police Department's Vice Squad at English Turn, and various other district stations and the St. Bernard Parish Sheriff's Office. Johnny Frederic, Tommy Tizzard, and Steve Juneau would make a delivery to the Plaquemines Parish Sheriff's Office and then pass through New Orleans, where they would try to make it to the North Shore of Lake Pontchartrain to make deliveries at several agencies in St. Tammany Parish. Sheriff Champagne and I were to make a trip into the New Orleans Garden District to retrieve legal documents and items from a home. Loading the trailers with fresh uniforms and personal hygiene supplies, off we all went in three different directions.

After making a stop in Plaquemines Parish, Johnny Frederic drove through New Orleans, onto the desolate stretch of Interstate 10 that led toward the washed-away Twin Span

Bridges crossing Lake Pontchartrain. They then took the Highway 11 Bridge into St. Tammany Parish, a sprawling region that 213,000 people call home.

They drove down the worn-out dirt median, which was elevated about three feet higher than the roadway. With water lapping the truck and trailer on both sides, they wondered if they had made a wise decision in selecting their route. Dead animals were everywhere. They had no way of knowing what lay ahead. With nowhere to turn around and afraid that if they slowed down, they would get stuck in the median, they had no choice but to keep going. As they inched forward, Tommy Tizzard kept apologizing for selecting the route and getting them into such a precarious situation. Once they made it, however, a relieved Tizzard proclaimed there had never been a doubt in his mind they would make it.

A National Guard unit was camped at the base of the Highway 11 Bridge; they made their way across the bridge into St. Tammany Parish, stopping at the Slidell Police Department. The City of Slidell, a growing suburb of New Orleans to which people flocked for waterfront lots with easy access to a wide range of recreational activities, had received extensive damage, as Hurricane Katrina's storm surge rushed into Lake Pontchartrain, washing away homes near the lakeshore and spilling into thousands of homes well inland.

Many homes were constructed along a maze of canals that allowed each homeowner to have water access from the backyard to Lake Pontchartrain. The innermost areas of the canals in the Oak Harbor subdivision were clogged with tons of debris that was so thick a person could walk across it. But this wasn't just any debris; days before, it was the lumber and building materials that had made up the homes of many who now only had only cement slabs on their property.

Moving on, they made deliveries at the Mandeville Police Department, St. Tammany Parish Sheriff's Office and the Causeway Police Department. They received permission to cross the closed 24-mile-long Causeway Bridge, so they would not have to test fate by making a second journey across the median on Interstate 10 in New Orleans East. The North Shore had access from Interstates 59 and 12, which gave them the advantage of being able to get supplies, but it was obvious they were still struggling to get needed supplies.

Rounding up the Horses

St. Charles Sheriff's Lieutenant Pam Schmitt was reassigned to work with the SPCA to capture and remove animals from the devastated area, and take them to the La Mar Dixon Equestrian Center in Gonzales, Louisiana. Most of the pets had been left in flooded areas with no food or drinkable water. Most were becoming sick and acting unpredictably as they desperately searched for food.

The day before, Lieutenant Schmitt had been sent to the corner of Thailia Street and Washington Avenue in New Orleans to capture a horse. Located in a community of the city known as the Gert Town, the area is comprised of older homes, various businesses and Xavier University. There, a large red roan horse was standing neck-deep in water with human bodies floating near it. A group of Texas National Guardsmen had unsuccessfully thrown wheat crackers to the horse, trying to get it to come close enough for capture. Lieutenant Schmitt made several unsuccessful attempts to coax the horse close enough to rope, but each time she got close, the horse would pull away and flee back into the water toward Thailia Street, as if he were expecting the rescuers to follow. Early in the morning the next day, with more protective gear and with experienced horse handling friends, Karen and Wayne Gossett, a second attempt was more successful.

As they approached the horse, a military Black Hawk helicopter hovered in the area and tipped his blade repeatedly, using the prop wash to coax the horse closer to the rescuers. They were surprised, however, when the red roan led the rescuers to five other horses on a raised patch of ground, concealed behind buildings. It wasn't until all five horses had been picked up that the red roan allowed himself to be caught. After taking the horses to a veterinarian checkpoint near Children's Hospital, all six horses were taken to the La Mar Dixon Equine Center.

Meanwhile, at the Evacuation Shelter in the Eual J. Landry Middle School, next to the St. Charles Parish Courthouse, a touching reunion occurred, demonstrating just how complicated the evacuation of over a million people would be for many families. A New Orleans family had become separated as they fled their flooding home in separate vehicles. Traveling through water-covered streets, two sisters became separated from the rest of their family. In Jefferson Parish, the older sister was arrested on felony drug charges and taken to the Jefferson Parish lock-up, while the younger, 13-year-old sister was brought to the New Orleans International Airport to be evacuated with thousands of others who were being flown to various locations throughout the United States. Visibly upset and with no guardian, the 13-year-old was in a vulnerable state. Jefferson deputies at the airport contacted Major Sam Zinna at the St. Charles Sheriff's Office and asked for his help. Major Zinna decided to bring the girl to the St. Charles Parish Shelter, where she would be watched closely until she could be reunited with family.

At the Shelter, St. Charles Sheriff's Office Corporal Freddie Smith took an interest in the young girl's predicament, and worked with her to try and locate family members. Unfortunately, the only telephone numbers and addresses the young girl knew were for the flooded homes in New Orleans from which she and her family had fled only days before. Corporal Smith kept a watchful eye over the young girl, keeping her off the daily buses that took evacuees to Baton Rouge for further travel and placement in other shelters.

Around 4:00 P.M., a very emotional mother arrived at the Eual J. Landry Shelter, carrying a photo of her missing daughter. She handed it to Corporal Smith. The exhausted, distraught woman had visited several shelters in the region, desperately searching for her 13-year-old daughter. Each time, she was turned away in what was beginning to resemble a hopeless effort. Immediately recognizing the young girl's photograph, Corporal Smith invited the mother into the shelter so she could look around. Almost immediately, the mother and daughter made eye contact and ran towards each other and embraced. After seeing nothing but fear and misery on the faces of those passing through the shelters, this reunion offered hope and a brighter day.

In retrospect, everyone who experienced the miseries of Hurricane Katrina will carry with them vivid memories of the ordeal. Corporal Smith remembers this special moment as the one Katrina memory he will hold onto as long as he lives.

Turning the Corner

Many of the 300 officers nationwide who responded to the disaster had done so for a one-week tour. Each day, officers were leaving for their long journey back home. They were leaving with much more than they had brought with them; each was a changed person. They had seen firsthand the devastation and suffering, to an extent that photographs and news reports could never fully capture. They had witnessed how law enforcement throughout the country united and helped stabilize a region left crippled by the worst natural disaster to strike the United States. A small handful took something else with them—Hurricane Katrina victims. Giving them Cajun names like Boudreaux, Marie, and Pierre, several officers took home with them new additions to their families: pets they had rescued from certain death as they wandered through contaminated floodwaters in search of food.

Although our manpower needs were less than they had been just five days earlier, we still needed additional officers for the following week's assignments. One option was to put out another call for assistance, but that had the potential to overwhelm us with more help than was needed. All we really needed was an additional 30 or so officers, to help with non-glamorous yet vital assignments. Almost as if someone were listening to my thoughts, my cell phone rang. On the other end was Jefferson County Sheriff's Chief Deputy Michael Hettich, calling from Louisville, KY, and asking how we were making out. A fellow member of the National Fraternal Order of Police Board, Chief Hettich had visited the area many times and had a personal connection to New Orleans. He was calling on behalf of Sheriff John Aubrey, who wanted to know if we still needed help. He promised that a team of 24 Jefferson County Deputies would arrive in one day, and a second team of 23 would later be sent to Plaquemines Parish to help with their recovery efforts as well.

Again that day, we would break up into groups and

travel in different directions, making supply deliveries. Johnny Frederic and Pete Bourque again traveled to the North Shore. Storms generally cause destruction near the coastline and 60 miles or so inland, as the costal marsh allows tidal surge to inundate communities. North of the potential storm surge, winds diminish rapidly when storms lose their punch as they interact with land, trees, and structures, and leave the warm waters of the Gulf of Mexico, their source of energy. Hurricane Katrina would again prove she was different. Her devastation had crippled a region roughly the size of England.

Johnny Frederic commented that he had never seen so much destruction over such a vast area this far inland. Both Franklinton and Bogalusa, Louisiana, with a combined population of 44,000, lay 120 miles inland from where the eye came on shore, and if the storm had lost any of its ferociousness before reaching these towns, it sure did not show. He spoke of the stories from those who live in this community, whose major industry is harvesting timber. It's dubbed "the land of the fallen pines." He explained how survivors spoke of the frightening sounds of the wind howling and the crashing sound as the trees fell, twisted, and snapped while the residents huddled in their damaged homes in fear, wondering if the next falling tree would crush them. After the storm passed, people had to climb across acres of toppled trees, which covered roadways for miles.

At the New Orleans Police Department Seventh District, which had set up a temporary district station inside a reception hall on Chef Menteur Blvd., a couple of female New Orleans Police officers approached the two U.S. Mint female officers, Lieutenant Ella Brooks and Officer Anna Lopez, and expressed the need for women's underwear and feminine hygiene products. When they returned to Destrehan High School that evening,

Lieutenant Brooks and Officer Lopez went to Wal-Mart and spent $100 of their own money to get these items for the female officers. These same items were available in our supply cache at the Baton Rouge Lodge and could have been delivered the next morning. Instead, Lieutenant Brooks and Officer Lopez, with their personal connection to these female New Orleans Police officers, would not accept reimbursement for their purchase. It really makes me proud to see law enforcement officers giving to other law enforcement officers in need.

Louisiana State Lodge Attorney Claude Schlesinger needed to retrieve files from his office in New Orleans for a Civil Service Hearing in Thibodaux, LA, and for other law enforcement cases. Schlesinger and his wife, Mimi, had left for Chicago to visit family on the Friday morning before the storm, when forecasters still had the storm headed for the Florida Panhandle. Because the storm wasn't threatening New Orleans when he left, he had not taken any storm precautions before leaving.

Sergeant Warren Lebeauf and myself accompanied Schlesinger to the Entergy Building on Loyola Avenue. There, with only partial power restored to the building, we ascended 25 flights of stairs. In the heat and humidity of a stairwell, the climb was a difficult and unpleasant one. Halfway up, we met up with a female National Guardsman, who was walking down from the building's roof as she toted a rifle that was as big as she was. Although she had carried it up the stairs earlier that day, gravity was working to her advantage on the way down. Twenty-five stories above the city, however, offered an interesting vantage point from which to survey the flooding. The north-facing window of Schlesinger's office was cracked, but had held in place. When it was time to leave and with my digital camera pressed against the window, I asked them to give me a few more minutes to take in the view. What I really wanted to do was catch my breath from the climb.

Once back on the ground, we passed by a few district stations in New Orleans and went to the Jefferson Parish Sheriff's Office. Each day, progress was visible. Volunteers on some of the main thoroughfares were cleaning up trash and debris. Flooded cars were being removed from the roadways and shoulders. More importantly, National Guardsmen and police officers were at every corner. Guardsmen could be seen moving about the city with convoys of equipment. Foot patrols walked the neighborhoods that had been pumped dry, and walked door-to-door, checking for bodies. Officers from visiting law enforcement agencies also patrolled the streets. Pick-up trucks, with officers brandishing rifles seated in the back, patrolled the streets en masse.

Adding to the growing number of National Guardsmen deployed, Federal Law Enforcement officers began pouring into the region. FBI, Immigrations and Customs, Drug Enforcement, Border Patrol, Fish and Wildlife Service Officers, and more all began augmenting a very tired and fatigued New Orleans Police Department. For the first time in New Orleans' 300-year history, the police outnumbered the general public. New Orleans had turned the corner, after two weeks of unspeakable horrors and an overwhelmed public safety system. The city's first responders could breathe a sigh of relief.

There was one very obvious concern, however. Every one of us noticed it, and it impacted virtually every agency and district station we visited. Everywhere we went, it was the same thing: every officer had the same look. Their lives were uncertain. If you want to see the look, it's easy to find. Walk into any hospital critical care waiting room and look into the faces of the family members as they wait and pray for their loved one, not knowing what the final outcome will be. Some laugh, some cry, some pray, and some just stare off into space, but all know that their lives have changed. They all have very little control of what lies ahead.

The difference is that when it's time to leave, the people in the waiting room will go to the sanctuaries of their homes, familiar surroundings and the people they love. The majority of these officers had no homes, and their love ones had been evacuated miles away. All they had was each other, and the camaraderie was unbelievable.

That evening, Mike Haley and I drove to Baton Rouge to meet with Jerry Gardiner, manager of the Southern Law Enforcement Foundation, a law enforcement peer counseling group that operates out of the Louisiana Fraternal Order of Police Office in Baton Rouge. Gardiner had also spent time in New York after the terrorist attacks on the World Trade Center, working with law enforcement officers as a peer counselor. Sitting in a closed McDonald's restaurant, we reviewed and coordinated peer-counseling efforts for the region.

Interestingly, we had never envisioned the Southern Law Enforcement Foundation as a relief organization. Their mission is to provide Critical Incident Stress Interventions at police incidents, not natural disasters. There was no written plan to go by, and no central command to assure the relief effort was providing for the needs. It was a handful of men and women dedicated to helping their brothers and sisters, working from a pure sense of service and using common sense as the compass.

Unlike the general population, where a call is made for help with an expectation of someone responding to fix the problem, cops are normally the responders, and by trade are resourceful. All they need is the opportunity to make things happen. As New Orleans Police officers made their way out of the city to the Belmont Hotel in Baton Rouge for debriefing before they could begin the furloughs, many went to the Police Shelter at the Baton Rouge Fraternal Order of Police Lodge, or to the Louisiana State Police Academy, where cots had been set up in the gym. The Southern Law Enforcement Foundation provided crisis intervention services to those who requested them, but more often that not, their primary function became helping officers reunite with their families.

Most officers were suffering from a feeling of isolation, and frustration from not knowing the location and condition of their families. The greatest stress on these officers was the innumerable, unanswerable questions they had inside. Once their families were settled in somewhere, so they didn't have to worry about them, their next level of concern centered on where they were going to sleep, and how they would get their meals, and showers. It didn't seem like much, but it was probably all they could absorb at that time.

Cops are resilient. It is hard to imagine an average person being able to go to work under such conditions. Jerry Gardiner mentioned that he had mistakenly thought he was going to the police shelters to provide critical stress interventions when, in fact, a ham sandwich and a Coke, a pat on the back, the use of a cell phone, a ride to the store, and a place to air their frustration was all they needed.

Our plan as we moved forward would be just as it started out. The Fraternal Order of Police would continue the relief supply efforts, providing food, water, clothes, and money to the hundreds of officers in New Orleans, and the Foundation would continue to set up sites where they could come into contact with first responders coming off duty. Without a disaster response plan prior to Hurricane Katrina's arrival, this combination of efforts would later be determined to resemble a textbook model of efficiency and continuity of services.

Listening to the radio that same day, on the way back to Destrehan High School, former Secretary of State Colin Powell was quoted from an interview on a popular national news program, 20/20. He criticized the response to Hurricane Katrina at all levels of the government, saying, "When you look at those who weren't able to get out, it should have been a blinding flash obvious to everybody that when you order a mandatory evacuation, you can't expect everybody to evacuate on their own. These are people who don't have credit cards; only one in 10 families at that economic level in New Orleans have a car. So it wasn't a racial thing—but poverty disproportionately affects African-Americans in this country. And it happened because they were poor." Finally, I said to myself, a voice of reason!

Day Fifteen
Friday, September 9, 2005

Catching our Breath

The headlines of the New Orleans Times Picayune read "Death toll may not be as high as feared." On the same page was news that the breaches at the 17th Street Canal and London Street Canal Systems were successfully closed. With floodwaters no longer flowing into the city, pumps were working much more efficiently and water was receding.

That morning, under the supervision of Major Wayne Lovan, 24 Jefferson County Sheriff's Deputies arrived at Destrehan High School from Louisville, Kentucky. They wasted no time in getting settled in and reporting for duty. With most of the initial volunteers gone or preparing to leave for home, they were a godsend. Without hesitation, they not only accepted the often-mundane crowd control assignments at hurricane assistance and distribution centers, retail outlets, and chemical facilities, but they actually took ownership in the recovery efforts. Through their own initiative, they improved upon the operations by better utilizing resources to make the storm victims more comfortable. With already frustrated storm victims being placed at ease, their efforts kept everything moving smoothly.

A second team of 22 Jefferson County Deputies would arrive days later in Plaquemines Parish under the supervision of Major Earl Droddy. They readily accepted the responsibility of working traffic checkpoints, relief supply centers, and the like. They, like many other out-of-state volunteer law enforcement officers, were giving overwhelmed and tired first responders an opportunity to catch their breath.

Lenny Whetsel, Gabe Kitka and the U.S. Mint Police set out for New Orleans, making deliveries at stations in New Orleans. As Lenny traveled down one street, a young black man was holding an object over his head and running directly at them, despite the strobe lights on their vehicle. They drew their weapons and waited. All of a sudden, the man stopped, looked at them, and smashed a beer bottle in front of them as he walked off. Within seconds, there were numerous gunshots being fired in their general area. They didn't stick around to find out what was happening; they got the hell out of the area.

That morning, Sheriff Champagne, Lieutenant Lee, Deputy Tim Fitzpatrick, and myself traveled to St. Bernard Parish with several Lafourche Parish officials who planned to cook a meal for the St. Bernard Parish employees. We had an additional passenger: a reporter with the Wall Street Journal, who asked if he could hitch a ride with us. Arriving in a warehouse at the Port of St. Bernard, people crowded in and sat on bundles of plywood delivered by a cargo ship only days before the storm. They explained their isolation and the many challenges they had trying to get outside support.

Leaving the warehouse, we passed by Lieutenant Lee's home. He had explained the damage to his home, but this was the first time I had actually seen it. By then, the floodwaters had drained, and the extreme heat had dried everything in the

Chest Deep and Rising:

sun. On the grass, streets, and driveway, the two-inch-thick coating of sludge had dried and cracked into small pieces that had curled, resembling a drought-stricken landscape. As we walked across the driveway, the dried sludge cracked with a sound so loud it was deafening. His home was a recently constructed brick home with a watermark that showed a five-foot water level inside. Whatever the water and wind had not destroyed trapped moisture and the expanding ever-expanding mold growing inside the home certainly finished off. Nothing was salvageable.

By then, the remainder of the first wave of visiting officers in St. Charles Parish was preparing to leave. Having spent a week working in the region, it was time for them to return home to regular duty. In New Orleans, however, home would never be the same. A few thousand of the City's police officers, firefighters and emergency medics were preparing to go home as well, but with their homes destroyed by the storm, home was a cramped cruise ship cabin. Two cruise ships were brought in and docked near the Julia Street wharf, where many first responders would live for months. In Plaquemines Parish, Sheriff Hingle had brought in mobile homes for his homeless deputies. They were parked under a row of weathered oak trees, near a government complex. Locals dubbed the row of mobile homes "Cop Land."

Late that day, I spoke with Major Roland Ladreyt, who mentioned a couple of interesting events that had unfolded in the preceding days. He explained how agents with the Louisiana Attorney General's Office had brought a doctor to the Tulane Medical Center to retrieve very valuable research materials and frozen cultures he had taken years to develop. The research would have no monetary value to a looter, but was invaluable in terms of its research. He also explained how agents on vehicle patrols had given chase to looters driving in a vintage Rolls Royce. With most of the city flooded and impassable, making their flight short-lived, the looters abandoned the vehicle and fled on foot. The agents were able to track down the vehicle's owner, and were told that legendary actress Lucile Ball had once owned the classic automobile. Needless to say, they were very happy to have the undamaged vehicle returned to them. These were but two more stories added to a growing list of unusual events surfacing in the strange world Hurricane Katrina had created.

Joe Joe Dancer

St. Charles Sheriff's Office Lieutenant Pam Schmitt received another animal rescue request, in which she was told dogs were attacking a horse. Packs of domestic dogs had banded together in search of food. Animal rescue groups were attempting to throw as many bags of food as they could throughout the area to feed the dogs, but the sheer number of stray animals made it a daunting task. Along with St. Charles Sheriff's Office Reserve Deputy Roy Gautreaux, and Jason Williams, a friend, Lieutenant Schmitt went to the 2900 block of Monteque Street near St Claude Avenue in New Orleans.

Jason rode in the back of the pick-up truck and when he saw a pack of dogs, he would split open and throw a bag of food towards the dogs. The dogs were skeptical at first, but once they smelled the food, they would violently attack the bag, throwing food everywhere as they competed for it amongst each other. When they arrived at Monteque Street, they saw a horse standing near a clump of trees with several dogs surrounding it. The fatigued and starving horse saw the horse trailer being pulled behind Lieutenant Schmitt's truck; he started neighing and pawing the ground as if the Calvary had just arrived, and in the nick of time. Jason split food bags open and threw them toward the dogs, to keep them at bay. As Lieutenant Schmitt opened the trailer door and Deputy Gautreaux guided the horse towards the trailer, with a burst of energy the frail little horse, with its bloody leg, leaped into the trailer and looked back at Lieutenant Schmitt as if to say, "SHUT THE DAMN DOOR."

The horse immediately started eating the hay they had placed inside the trailer. After a while, his eye closed, as if asleep for the first time in weeks. He was taken to the La Mar Dixon Equine Center. As they unloaded the little horse, a young man who was assisting with the animals called for his father to come and take a look at this particular horse. As the older man walked up slowly, looking at the horse, he said, "That's Joe Joe Dancer!" The son nodded in agreement. He asked where the horse had been picked up. Hearing the answer, petting the horse, both men nodded while saying in a soothing voice, "Yeah, this is Joe Joe Dancer." In her haste, Lieutenant Schmitt had to depart without learning the story of Joe Joe Dancer.

Seventeen unclaimed horses, including Joe Joe Dancer, would later be adopted by a farm in Northern Louisiana, where the owner intends to allow these forgotten Hurricane Katrina victims to live out their days in peace.

Lieutenant Schmitt would undertake a huge task over the next few weeks. She and other volunteers brought horses, dogs, cats, chickens, ducks, and even a swan to the La Mar Dixon Equine Center over a four-week period.

Day Sixteen
Saturday, September 10, 2005

Down in Plaquemines

Two weeks after Hurricane Katrina made landfall in the small Plaquemines Parish community of Empire, Louisiana, and two weeks later than promised, I visited Plaquemines Parish to drop off supplies. A thin sliver of land that protrudes south into the Gulf of Mexico, Plaquemines Parish is home to 29,000 people, mostly fishermen and oil production workers. I made contact with Colonel Charles Guey and apologized for not keeping my promise to call the day after the storm to see how he had made out. He laughed and told me his experiences during the early days of Hurricane Katrina. Colonel Guey explained that after speaking with me by cell phone only hours before Hurricane Katrina's arrival, he had made his way from the Communications Building in Port Sulphur to Belle Chasse, where he and just over 100 Sheriff's Office and public works employees had ridden out the storm on the second floor of the Belle Chasse High School.

When the winds started to diminish, he and Plaquemines Sheriff Jiff Hingle ventured out to survey the damage. Something caught their eyes—driftwood on the highway. Driftwood and tidal surge had been pushed over the Mississippi River levee, leaving piles of debris covering the top and landside of the levee. The surge was not large enough to have caused any serious flooding, at least not in Belle Chasse. They continued south into the Jesuit Bend community, where the homes did not escape Hurricane Katrina's floodwaters. Water ranging from a few inches to five feet had inundated homes. Further south in the Myrtle Grove area, the highway was flooded. This ended the survey by land.

At Belle Chasse High School, a search and rescue team had been established. With four airboats in tow, they left Belle Chasse and again made their way south to Myrtle Grove. The further south they traveled, the trickier driving became. The highway was littered with trees, boats, and debris at the time. The winds were still blowing above 50 mph, and higher in gusts; rain was intermittent and heavy at times.

With all four boats in the water and underway, their first stop was at a home in an area known as Pointe Celeste. The homeowner and some friends had decided to ride out Hurricane Katrina at his sturdy brick house, built at the elevation of the levee so that flooding would not be an issue. It wasn't; they were all fine. They continued south, to a doublewide mobile home in the community of West Pointe-a-la-hache. There, a family of eight had foolishly decided to ride out Hurricane Katrina in a mobile home, and were now in five feet of water. Of the family, the youngest was four years old and the eldest 82. They were rescued and taken to higher ground.

Captain Robert Cosse carefully piloted his boat and maneuvered between the displaced houses, vehicles, power lines, and now ruptured natural gas lines. As they continued traveling south, Sergeant Michael Martin shouted, "Duck! Wire." There was a low-hanging power line, shoulder high to a seated passenger in the airboat. Sergeant Martin, who was riding on the bow, dove down into the boat. As he went down, he could see the power line headed directly for them. Two other deputies dove down as well. Colonel Guey went down, just missing the line. He landed right on top of the rest of them. The wire struck the pipe behind them and slid over Captain Cosse, who immediately stopped the boat. After taking a few minutes to compose themselves, they headed south again, more alert, and even more aware of the dangers.

As they continued south to "St. Jude Hump," a ring levee, they all stared in shock. The area that had never flooded in the past was now completely under water, with roofs of homes and buildings protruding out of the water. Looking for survivors, they moved into the community of Diamond, where they found five people who had ridden out the storm in their home. The survivors explained how they saw the water coming and tried to go to the Mississippi River levee, higher ground, but didn't make it. They had their life jackets on and hung on to a tree until the winds calmed down, then swam back to the house to wait for help. Loaded into the boats, the survivors were taken to the levee they had previously tried to reach. They were given drinking water and told they would be picked up on the return trip.

Colonel Guey explained that having lived and worked in this part of the parish all his life, he thought he should have been able to recognize his surroundings, but this was not the case. Except for a few landmarks, such as street signs or the tops of certain buildings, there was no way to tell exactly where he was at any given time. The wind and the water had moved most homes and businesses from their original locations. Now, there were part of the highways, streets, or canals. Some homes had moved as much as a mile and a half from their foundations, while others had simply vanished.

Chest Deep and Rising:

This was the case as they made their way though the community of Port Sulphur, dodging buildings, utility poles, wire and submerged vehicles. There, they encountered the strong odor of crude oil. Several oil storage tanks had been displaced by the storm, and the oil that was once held in the tanks was now coating the floodwater and everything in the area. In Port Sulphur, two men were stranded on the roof of a house in the Hayes Subdivision. Dropping them off on the levee, the rescue crew located a third man, stranded on a roof surrounded by power lines. The houses were corralled like cattle, and the airboats were having difficulty reaching the man. A Coast Guard helicopter crew passing by saw the man, dropped its basket, and plucked him from the roof.

They continued on to Civic Drive and saw that the floodwater had completely inundated the Sheriff's Office's 911 Communications Center. Even though the water was then only four to five feet deep, the watermark visible on the exterior of the building indicated that the floodwaters had reached a depth of four feet on the second floor of the well-constructed building. As they turned the corner to approach the school, the school's coach and his friends began waving frantically at them. Colonel Guey explained how the night before he had tried to get them to evacuate, but they refused. Climbing into the boat, the coach smiled at Guey and said, "Don't say a word."

The rescue crew then proceeded to their next stop, the parish government building, where they noticed that the parking lot was littered with flooded vehicles that had been rearranged by the rushing tidal surge. They also noticed a pickup truck resting on top of one of the building's air conditioning units, perfectly balanced. Over a dozen parish employees had ridden out the storm on the building's second floor. It took each boat two trips to move everyone. After dropping off their precious cargo, the rescuers headed south, toward St. Patrick's Church, where Sheriff Hingle's boat had arrived several minutes prior. As the engine on the boat stopped, they were surprised to see Sheriff Hingle emerge from the church, standing in over five feet of water. One by one, he helped the six people who had found refuge in the church choir loft onto the awaiting boats. While at the church, one of the survivors explained that there were two people at a home near the church. The partially submerged homes were located; they circled both houses, calling for survivors, but got no response.

They stayed as long as they could and then had to leave the area, because fuel was running low. Reluctantly, they started north, checking for survivors as they returned to Myrtle Grove. When they got to the St. Jude Hump, they were surprised to see that the Coast Guard had dropped several survivors off on the levee as well. It took some shuffling, but they were able to get everyone into a boat to make their way north. By the time the day was over, 54 survivors had been rescued. In the days that followed, trips were made further south, where more survivors were rescued.

Colonel Guey explained to us that the first outside help had arrived on the Thursday after the storm. It was not what one would expect, however. The assistance was not FEMA or the National Guard, or any federal agency. With an expression of both anger and appreciation, an emotional Colonel Guey explained that the help had come from his brothers and sisters in the law enforcement community. The first to arrive were members of the Louisiana Fraternal Order of Police, who brought clothing and hygiene products for his deputies. That same afternoon, they received word that Tuscaloosa County Alabama Sheriff Ted Sexton, President of the National Sheriff's Association, would be in the parish that evening. Arriving with him would be several Sheriff's Office members, including the Hennepin County Sheriff's Office, whose deputies arrived with a mobile command center. This command center helped to re-establish much-needed communications.

With tremendous pride, Colonel Guey explained that through all this, the brave men and women of the Plaquemines Parish Sheriff's Office had remained at their posts before, during, and after Hurricane Katrina, even though over 70% of them had lost their homes. They had only the clothes on their backs to claim.

During our visit, as we drove south into Lower Plaquemines Parish, occasionally maneuvering around buildings and boats that had come to rest in the middle of Highway 23, Colonel Guey often pointed to vacant land, explaining the types of buildings that had stood at these locations just two weeks earlier. I was in awe at the level of destruction. I was amazed that anyone could have survived it. The fact that the death toll in Plaquemines Parish was so low was a tribute to emergency preparedness planners and residents who understood their vulnerability and the need to evacuate.

Only able to travel as far south as Port Sulphur because of flooding that day, I witnessed some of the worst destruction I had seen in the entire region. I gazed into what had become open fields: steps, slabs, and pillars represented the many homes and structures that had been completely washed from their foundations. Communication towers lay mangled in piles of rubble; coffins washed from their cemeteries had been gathered and placed next to the government complex.

Johnny Frederic had departed that morning for the long trip to Grand Isle, located at the southernmost tip of Jefferson Parish. The island had been severely damaged by strong winds and a massive tidal surge that covered the island and all the roads leading to it. The island's bridge that connects the seven mile island to the mainland was damaged and cut off to vehicular traffic. There he delivered supplies and BDU uniforms to the grateful Grand Isle Police Department. They, too, had been cut off from communications, supplies, and outside assistance for over a week until water receded enough to allow vehicles to reach the island.

As I headed back home at the end of that day, the region, although crippled, seemed to have stabilized. State and Federal services and supplies began to arrive. With the help of National Guard Troops and visiting law enforcement, calmness settled over a ravaged region. This difficult moment in time will be forever known as the 16-day nightmare called Hurricane Katrina. Although many challenges awaited us at every corner during the days that followed, for the many victims of Hurricane Katrina, each day would be better than the day before.

Day Seventeen
Sunday, September 11, 2005

Moment of Reflection

The start of Sunday, September 11th began with somber reflection on the significance of this date four years earlier. It marked the day we learned the true price of freedom and the depths of hatred. Yet it is also the day Americans pulled together and showed the world the true tenacity of our sprit. On that dreadful day in 2001, the world saw death and destruction like never before, when terrorists flew commercial airplanes into the Twin Towers of the World Trade Center in New York, the Pentagon in Virginia, and crashed in a corn field in Pennsylvania. The death and destruction shocked the world and crippled a nation. From what appeared to be our weakest moment emerged unmatched strength. This was strength far greater than our nation had ever before witnessed. If the terrorists thought their hatred would collapse a nation, they had made one serious underestimation. America is not a building, nor is it a landmark. No; what they failed to recognize is that America is the spirit of our people.

How ironic, I thought, my senses numb from the events and challenges I had witnessed in the previous 16 days.

Chest Deep and Rising:

The two events don't compare, but they have some common ingredients. In both, innocent people died. And in both, American's planners and responders revealed just how unprepared it is to prevent disasters. Yet, in both, no matter how much despair we felt at our lowest points, life goes on… we pick up the pieces, and in doing so, we learn a little more about who we really are.

At Destrehan High School, most of the remaining volunteers were packing their gear into their vehicles for the journey back home. With them, they took endless stories of their experiences and observations. But equally as important, they took with them the feeling that they had truly made a difference in the lives of so many who had lost everything. Just like those living in the affected region, their lives, too, are forever changed. After expressing my gratitude and appreciation and saying our goodbyes, it was back to work. With about 50 volunteers remaining for another week, there was still much to be done.

We passed by the New Orleans Steamship Wharf and met with Lieutenant Henry Dean, who explained that a directive from the New Orleans Police "top brass" asked that our deliveries directly to the districts end. All donated supplies were to be brought to a special staging area in the warehouse district, and the department would distribute the supplies themselves. Passing by the warehouse, it was clear that supplies were making it to the city, and there was a plan in place to supply the first responders. It was also clear, from the volume of supplies in this warehouse, that the need for our daily supply runs into New Orleans was diminishing.

Back in St. Charles Parish, things were progressing well. Businesses were reopening, power was restored, and schools were readying to reopen. Things were improving in the region... We had turned the corner.

PART THREE

Hurricane Rita Tests Shattered Nerves

It wouldn't take long for nerves to be tested once more. Three weeks after Hurricane Katrina forever changed southeast Louisiana and southern Mississippi, Hurricane Rita added insult to injury as she flooded areas already devastated by Katrina. Rita also claimed communities shown mercy by Hurricane Katrina and started the whole process over again.

Like a sequel to a really bad movie, Hurricane Katrina's big sister, Hurricane Rita, entered the Gulf, and it too promised to keep everyone on the edge of their seats a bit longer. Three weeks after Hurricane Katrina made landfall, New Orleans Mayor Ray Nagin announced his plan to repopulate his evacuated city. Mother Nature, however, had other plans. The reopening was cancelled, and a re-evacuation of the city was initiated only three days later as Hurricane Rita, by now the strongest storm on record, was initially forecasted to make landfall close to the City of New Orleans.

Although Hurricane Rita remained well to the south and west of New Orleans, the pre-landfall storm surge she brought created interesting challenges to the fragile and already compromised levee system. Parts of the city that had been pumped dry were again filling with floodwaters, caused by the strong winds that plagued the area for days as Hurricane Rita skirted

Chest Deep and Rising:

the Louisiana coastline. In the southern portions of Lafourche and Terrebonne Parishes, just 40 miles south-southwest of New Orleans, hundreds of homes that had escaped Hurricane Katrina's fury were flooded by Hurricane Rita.

Retired Lake Charles Police Officer Randy Bellon, a member of the Louisiana State Lodge Fraternal Order of Police board, evacuated ahead of Hurricane Rita. He and his family moved into the Louisiana State Lodge office in Baton Rouge. Only days before, the Tizzard family had returned to their Jefferson Parish homes, after living in the office for weeks.

When Hurricane Rita made landfall on the Louisiana and Texas border, the strongest winds and highest tidal surge were on the Louisiana side of the landfall. The larger populated areas of Galveston and Houston were spared the storm surge when Hurricane Rita struck farther east. Winds blowing offshore in Texas actually flattened the surge, which was only seven feet, well below the height of the Galveston seawalls that protect the city. The expected rainfall of five inches in New Orleans also did not happen, and the pressure on the levee system was eased. Still, storm surges of 15–20 feet struck southwestern Louisiana and the coastal parishes there. Damage in southwestern Louisiana was extensive.

In Cameron Parish, the communities of Hackberry, Cameron, Creole, Grand Chenier, and Holly Beach were heavily damaged or entirely destroyed. A riverboat casino and several barges broke loose from their moorings in Lake Charles and damaged an Interstate 10 bridge crossing the Calcasieu River. Lake Charles experienced severe flooding, with reports of water rising six to eight feet in areas around the lake itself. Damage to the city's electrical system was so severe that authorities warned that power would not return for weeks.

It is estimated that well over two million customers

lost power at the hands of Hurricane Rita. Total damage is estimated at $9.4 billion, making Rita the ninth-costliest storm in U.S. history. Thanks to Hurricanes Rita and Katrina, the entire coast of Louisiana lay in ruins, with Rita placing even greater demands on an already-burdened state and federal disaster response. However, the lessons learned by Hurricane Katrina meant that evacuations were more efficient and resources more accessible, making the response and recovery of Hurricane Rita a little more organized. It was, however, no less devastating for those who lived in her path of destruction.

Once the winds died down, Johnny Frederic and Randy Bellon made repeated trips to southwest Louisiana, delivering supplies to law enforcement officers. However, state and federal assistance arrived much sooner, making the Fraternal Order of Police efforts short-term.

The Power of Human Kindness

All across America, Fraternal Order of Police Lodges were pulling together and helping their counterparts in Louisiana and Mississippi by raising funds, collecting supplies, and assisting law enforcement families. With an estimated 2,000 law enforcement officers left homeless, the National Fraternal Order of Police's Disaster Relief Fund provided over $850,000.00 in direct financial assistance to the law enforcement officers who lost their homes. Add to this the supplies the organization purchased, and the total exceeded $1 million in Fraternal Order of Police Disaster Relief Aid.

The Louisiana Fraternal Order of Police offered a wide range of services, from opening a police family shelter to daily deliveries of supplies. They created a support network for law enforcement families, by funneling messages between families and officers separated in the evacuation and assisting in reuniting them. They also developed a Critical Incident Response Network, and they fed hundreds of law enforcement officers daily. In the recovery stages, they hired a construction contractor to work exclusively on the homes of law enforcement officers.

In addition, the Fraternal Order of Police helped coordinate the deployment of volunteer law enforcement personnel from agencies all across the United States to affected areas; this allowed officers to take time off to reunite with their own families and make repairs to their damaged homes. It is heartwarming to see how we have all pulled together and made a difference.

The day after Hurricane Katrina struck, Special Agent Linda Law, with the Louisiana Attorney General's Office, began receiving calls of assistance from members of the International Association of Women Police, of which she is an active member. The first call that she received was from Captain Christine Murray of the Orange County Sheriff's Department, who immediately sent 1,000 police t-shirts and four satellite telephones. The t-shirts were distributed to first responders in Jefferson and Orleans Parishes. The satellite phones were used by the Louisiana Department of Justice and the Jefferson Parish Sheriff Department, to assist in the coordination of efforts at a time when all other means of communications were inoperable.

The following week, Captain Murray organized a drive, collecting bulletproof vests, boots, uniforms, cots, blankets, food, generators, and gloves for the Jefferson Parish Sheriff Department. Deputies from Orange County, California, drove a refrigerated 18-wheeler to the Jefferson Parish Detective Bureau and donated the container and its contents to the Jefferson Parish Sheriff's Office. Other supplies came in from the organizations and were distributed throughout the New Orleans metro area, and eventually to west Louisiana, following Hurricane Rita. The supplies came from all over the United States, Canada and Australia.

At the Astrodome, members of the Houston Fraternal Order of Police walked through the shelter, holding a sign, searching for family members of law enforcement officers to help them find temporary housing. In Atlanta, Georgia, Dekalb County Fraternal Order of Police Lodge #13 took in the family of a New Orleans Harbor Police officer. They helped find an apartment and furniture, and welcomed them into their communities. In Louisville, KY, a female New Orleans Police officer also had a new apartment for her family, thanks to the Deputy Sheriff's Lodge.

In the northwest, the Idaho Panhandle Fraternal Order of Police Lodge and Bonner County Sheriff Elaine Savage partnered to create Operation Backup. They coordinated a statewide effort to collect basic supplies needed for law enforcement personnel and their families. With relief supplies collected and loaded onto a rented U-Haul truck, they headed south. After delivering supplies to the Mississippi Gulf Coast, the deputies helped patrol St. Charles Parish.

The Indianapolis Police Department, the Indianapolis Fraternal Order of Police Lodge and Auxiliary Lodge teamed together to gather donations and supplies. The Indianapolis Police Department, Marion County Sheriff and several surrounding police agencies escorted three semi trucks. A semi trailer departing from Muncie, Indiana, loaded with medical supplies joined in on the convoy. A sea of blue and red lights steamed towards Jackson County, Mississippi, where the supplies were used in evacuation shelters. Similar efforts were being coordinated by a Federal Officers' lodge in New Jersey, the New York State Lodge, Minnesota State Lodge, and the California State Lodge. All collected supplies and sent them to Louisiana and Mississippi.

In Lexington, Lieutenant Claire Olsen Reilly, a retired New Orleans Police officer and the first female Lieutenant in the department, was experiencing pain from surgery she had endured only days before evacuating New Orleans. Evacuated

Chest Deep and Rising:

from her New Orleans home, Claire and her daughter, Kellie, had first stopped in Dallas, Texas, then Houston, and finally ended up in Lexington. She was recovering from knee surgery and had not begun physical therapy. In addition, she was also experiencing pain in her shoulder and wrist.

Traveling was extremely painful. Out of money and in a town where she knew no one, Claire went into a public library and e-mailed a friend in Louisiana, explaining her predicament, and asked for help. The message was forwarded to the Louisiana Fraternal Order of Police. A couple of phone calls later, and Detective Joe Hess with the Blue Grass Fraternal Order of Police Lodge in Lexington and Kentucky National Fraternal Order of Police Trustee Michael Hettich were knocking on her door. The Blue Grass Lodge adopted her and her daughter, and helped by securing housing and employment for Kellie. Claire began physical therapy and the two of them have settled into Lexington with an ever-increasing list of new friends.

When the Jefferson County Sheriff's Office Rapid Response Team from Louisville, Kentucky, was deployed to St. Charles Parish to help in recovery efforts, the personal side of the storms' victims affected them. Such was the case with Detective Joey Thibodeaux of the St. Charles Sheriff's Office. Detective Thibodeaux not only suffered the loss of almost all of his personal belongings when his Kenner, Louisiana, apartment flooded, but hours after Hurricane Katrina struck, he received word that his brother had passed away unexpectedly in California.

Riding on patrol with Detective Thibodeaux, some of the Jefferson County deputies were impressed with how, despite such personal tragedy and hardships, Detective Thibodaux remained positive and focused as he insisted on remaining on the job. When the Jefferson County deputies returned to Louisville and explained Detective Thibodeaux's hardships to their fellow members, the Jefferson Sheriff's Fraternal Order of Police Lodge sent assistance to him to help ease the financial burden of traveling to California.

Retired New Orleans Police officer John Isbell, his wife, Anne Marie, and three-year-old, Keaton, were forced from their home by floodwater and crude oil that spilled into the community when a large tank at an area refinery ruptured. Their home and all of their belongings were completely destroyed. Their only possessions were the clothes on their back. Following an introduction from the Louisiana Fraternal Order of Police, the Battlefield Fraternal Order of Police Lodge located in Manassas, Virginia, immediately began providing aid. They sent boxes of clothing to John and his family, and financial assistance to help the family cope with the difficult challenges of being separated from their home. Immediately after the storm, John stayed at a hotel in Baton Rouge, where he continued to work in the security field while his wife and son were living temporarily with friends in another city.

Having adopted John and his family, the Battlefield Lodge, Auxiliary and Associate Lodges held fundraisers in Manassas. As John and his family began the arduous task of rebuilding their lives, they weren't alone. Over 1,100 miles away from the destruction of Hurricane Katrina, fellow law enforcement officers, their families, and friends they had never met unselfishly helped the Isbell family rebound from the loss of their home.

The Ohio State Lodge Fraternal Order of Police reached out to the officers of the New Orleans Harbor Police and adopted those who were left homeless by Hurricane Katrina. They invited the Harbor Police officers to make a list of items needed to help their southern counterparts get back on their feet. The Ohio State Lodge shared this list with Ohio Lodges, which all kicked into action. Some donated money; others organized fundraisers. In Marion, Ohio, a small local Lodge hosted a "Dodge Ball Tournament," with the proceeds going to the cause. In all, the Ohio State Lodge provided over $10,000, plus items on the list to their counterparts in the Harbor Police Department.

As telephone lines were restored, St. Charles Parish Councilman Richard Duhe, a Norco, Louisiana resident, received a call from Cindi van der Sluys Veer, a resident of Norco, California. Weeks earlier, she, her husband, and their children were in New Orleans attending the National Fraternal Order of Police Conference when they noticed a boy wearing a Norco Baseball T-shirt. After a conversation with the boy, they learned that their hometown had a sister city nearly 2,000 miles away in Louisiana.

While watching weather reports of Hurricane Katrina's storm track as she bore down on the Louisiana coastline, she saw that Norco, Louisiana was in the path of Katrina. Later, watching news coverage of all the destruction Hurricane Katrina caused, she had to help and concentrated her efforts on assisting the schools in the Norco area.

Cindi contacted the Principal and the PTA at her children's school, Norco, (California) Elementary. They started a fund drive initially asking students for pocket change to support Norco Elementary, Norco Primary, and Sacred Heart of Jesus Catholic Schools, all three located in Norco, Louisiana. They added a pancake breakfast as a fundraiser. Norco, California newspapers got involved in helping to promote the fund drive. The Norco, California Mayor's Office and City Council joined in, as did Highland Elementary, Sierra Vista Elementary, Riverview Elementary, and Norco High School.

Their efforts resulted in collecting over $10,000 for the three schools in Norco, Louisiana. Councilman Duhe presented the checks on behalf of the schools and students of our sister city in California.

Hundreds of first responders from various agencies, many of them living on a cruise ship docked near the New Orleans Convention Center, were invited to celebrate Thanksgiving dinner at the St. Charles Fraternal Order of Police Lodge in Destrehan. Frank Ferreyra, president of the New York Fraternal Order of Police, hired a local caterer and provided a feast for his counterparts in the south. Having witnessed the death and destruction of the terrorist attacks on the World Trade Center and the outpouring of support a united nation offered, he wanted to return the favor. Ferreyra and Emil Braun, an associate Lodge member from New York, talked with officers who had survived Hurricane Katrina and spoke of the many similarities between the terrorist attacks and Hurricane Katrina. Ferreyra found satisfaction in providing comfort to hundreds of officers who had lost their homes. For the officers who attended the dinner, they found comfort in knowing others recognized their plight.

Located on the north shore of Lake Pontchartrain, the City of Slidell, Louisiana, suffered extensive destruction as Hurricane Katrina's tidal surge washed away homes along the lakeshore as if they were matchsticks. Further inland, rising water invaded thousands of homes, destroying a lifetime of memories that each family had collected over the years. Many of those left homeless were members of the Slidell Police Department. As Hurricane Katrina moved north, despite their own losses, these officers rescued residents trapped in flooded homes and assisted in the long, arduous task of rebuilding their community.

One of the officers impacted by Hurricane Katrina was Slidell Police Sergeant Daniel Schewe, the father of Dan Schewe, an officer with the Inkster Police Department, located in Michigan. This father and son connection was all that was needed to form a mission of compassion between two agencies over 1,030 miles apart from each other.

Under the direction of Officer Jim Donahue, the Metro Detroit Fraternal Order of Police Lodge took the names and contact information of individual Slidell officers who had lost most or all of their worldly possessions and paired them up with Michigan members, who "adopted" the Louisiana officers and their families. Creating a one-on-one relationship between officers of both agencies, the "Adopt-a-Cop" program was born. In all, 34 families in Slidell received assistance, which helped get their lives back in order, but just as importantly, every officer in both agencies now has a new appreciation of the power of friendship and the spirit of human kindness.

Divine Intervention

As New Orleanians began to return home from a month-long evacuation, DEA Group Supervisor Craig Wiles and DEA Drug Task Force member Lieutenant George Breedy were patrolling the streets of New Orleans, watchful for the thousands of homes and businesses left unattended by a population that had been dispersed throughout the country.

Following a radio conversation with other patrolling taskforce members about a warehouse on Bartholomew Street, they decided to take a ride over and meet up with other officers. While patrolling, a couple of Task Force members were flagged down by the owner of the old Frey warehouse that had been empty before the storm. However, upon her return to the city, she found her warehouse filled with food and bottled water, pallets full of the stuff. It appeared to be enough to feed an army, and it probably was. A National Guard unit had commandeered the large building and used it as their supply house while deployed in the city.

When the National Guard departed the city, they chose to leave their stockpile of food and water behind. The lady asked the officers if they knew of anyone who might need the supplies. With fresh memories of a time just weeks before when supplies and support were slow to make it into the city, they thought of how they would really have appreciated such an offer back then. Officers and warehouse owner alike couldn't help wondering why such a large amount of supplies would simply be abandoned. Promising they would pass the word around to see if anyone knew of a need, they proceeded on patrol.

Minutes later, something out of the ordinary caught the officers' eye at the intersection of St. Anthony and St. Claude Avenues. In that devastated area of New Orleans, where everything below the well-defined waterline had a grayish tint from a coating of sludge deposited by the tidal surge, they saw a nun, dressed in a full white and black habit, standing next to a van. A large number of people had gathered around her. Suspicious, they stopped and spoke to Sister Mary Cecilia, a Dominican nun with the Cathedral Academy, a school located next to the St. Louis Cathedral in the heart of the New Orleans French Quarter.

A man from New York, who had watched the tragedy unfold on his television at home and felt he had to help in any way he could, had driven his van to New Orleans, where he befriended the Dominican nuns. Together, they were handing out MREs to anyone who needed them. The items were at the Academy; the nuns felt others would have a greater need than they did.

Sister Mary Cecilia explained that with all the New Orleans Public Schools closed and with an uncertain reopening date, the Dominican nuns at Cathedral Academy had decided they would open their school and offer it tuition-free to any child returning to the city and wanting to learn. If the academy was to open, she explained, they needed safe drinking water. City Water had been reestablished in the area of the Academy, but there were concerns about health risks from drinking it.

The two officers glanced at each other with a grin. Telling the nun to follow them in their van, they drove straight to the Frey warehouse, where they loaded the van and several DEA vehicles with the bottled water left behind by the National Guard, and brought it to the Academy for the students to use. The two officers gave Sister Mary Cecilia their business cards, telling her to call if she needed anything, and they continued to patrol the desolate streets of New Orleans.

The next day, the officers received a call from Sister Mary Cecilia, who reminded them of their offer that she was to call if she needed help. Sister Mary Cecilia then explained that she needed a dumpster and a bike. Confused by the request, the officers went to the Academy to see what they could do. There, they learned that the dumpster was to be used to clean the school grounds of storm debris and make it a safe environment for students. The second request was for the school janitor, who had lost his only means of transportation when his bike was stolen during the tense days following the storm.

Perplexed as to where they might find a dumpster with most of the city still shut down, the two men sat in their patrol car and began talking about the difficulty of the request. With so much cleaning up to be done throughout the region, dumpsters would be at a premium. The two men started fumbling through their pockets for cash they were willing to donate for the rental of a dumpster. Lieutenant Breedy commented that what they really needed was a garbage truck, not a dumpster, but where would they get one?

While still in the Academy parking lot, they heard a familiar sound: the systematic roar of an engine, followed by the sounds of an air brake. The officers looked up and caught a brief glimpse of a garbage truck as it passed on the street outside the brick courtyard entrance to the school. Glancing at each other with another grin, they turned on their police lights and sped out of the school parking lot, and pulled the

Chest Deep and Rising:

garbage truck over a few blocks away. Explaining their unusual request to the relieved driver, the driver agreed to haul off all the trash. Returning to the Academy, everyone pitched in as the school ground was cleared of trash and hauled away.

Feeling pretty good about themselves, Lieutenant Breedy and Group Supervisor Wiles went back on patrol. They watched a man open a warehouse and stopped to check him out. After confirming the man indeed worked at the warehouse, they talked with him a while as he related his Hurricane Katrina nightmare. Out of the corner of their eyes, the officers watched two young women open the same warehouse door and push two bicycles inside. They asked the man if the women worked with him, and he explained that the women were with the "Bike Project." They receive recovered and abandoned bikes from throughout the city, refurbish them, and give them to needy children. The man explained that the warehouse owner allows them to use part of the warehouse as their workshop. Again, the two officers glanced at each other with a grin, and began to explain the request they had received from Sister Mary Cecilia. Minutes later, they were headed to Cathedral Academy with a bike hanging out of the patrol car.

The next day, the phone rang yet again, with another request. This time, the call was from Sister Mary Rose, the principal of the Cathedral Academy. She had ordered furniture and appliances from a local store, but the store was not making deliveries. She asked the officers to please make arrangements to have the furniture delivered to the Academy. With a couple of pick-up trucks and strong volunteers, they loaded the furniture and appliances. While doing so, they explained to the store manager the series of unusual coincidences that had occurred each time they were asked to help the nuns at Cathedral Academy. The manager walked off and returned with additional furniture items he decided to throw in for free. Again glancing at each other with a grin, they drove to the Academy.

Once there, the grinning came to an end. The officers' good luck had run out. As they carried the furniture up stairs and through hallways, they were forced to remove doors, frames and molding to get the oversized items inside.

Even when things seem the darkest, all that is needed is the selfless determination and desire to make life a little better for someone else. With that, everything else just seems to fall in place. Cathedral Academy was the first school, public or private, to reopen in Orleans Parish, and the Dominican nuns welcomed anyone with open arms.

A Disaster in the Planning

Why is it we never seem to have enough time or money to do things right, yet we always find the time and money to fix things when they break?

It had been nearly 40 years since a major storm struck the City of New Orleans. Hurricane Betsy made landfall in New Orleans in 1965. Since that time, storms have threatened the city, but each either resulted in a glancing blow or caused minimal effects as it passed near the coastline. When the skies are blue and the birds are singing, it is hard to engage support for increased levee protection and adequate evacuation plans. On August 29, 2005, America developed a newfound respect for the forces of Mother Nature, as Hurricane Katrina forever changed the thought processes of not only coastal communities, but of the entire nation.

Two weeks after Hurricane Katrina devastated the Gulf South, police and military patrolled the vacant streets in many southeast Louisiana parishes. In New Orleans, piles of debris covered the Convention Center and Superdome, and contaminated floodwater covered most of the city, shattered windows of looted stores and flooded vehicles lined the streets, several hundred flooded city buses lay in ruin inside their fenced compounds, and burned-out buildings all gave but a brief hint of the countless nightmares the region had experienced for the intense 16 days Hurricane Katrina had presented. How could something like this happen in America? Storms will always test our resolve, but the events that happened in the aftermath of Hurricane Katrina were preventable.

With nearly every local television and radio station knocked off the air, a shutdown of telephone and radio communications, tens of thousands of people stranded on rooftops trying to escape rising floodwaters, and looting and lawlessness rampant in the streets, elected officials of the rapidly flooding City of New Orleans found themselves trying to develop a plan of action at the height of the most costly natural disaster on record.

It is apparent that a major portion of resources at the state and federal level were focused on the New Orleans area, where the demands were tremendous. However, the demands of New Orleans overshadowed the needs of many affected communities that were equally vulnerable. The system is broken and needs fixing before it is tested again with another disaster.

The slow response was the result of a breakdown on all levels of government. Prior to Hurricane Katrina, large cities such as New Orleans had not developed realistic plans that would include evacuation in the event of an emergency. The fact that New Orleans, with its population of 462,000 people, has a 27.9% poverty level, much higher than the national average, only reaffirms that an even greater emphasis should have been placed on such an evacuation plan. Instead, city and state officials were trying to develop a plan in the middle of a crisis occurring live on every news network in the free world. The deteriorating conditions, and no visible plan to deal with them, gave way to hopelessness and despair: all the factors needed for a meltdown of society. These lessons would forever change the nation's thinking on large-scale evacuations.

There should not have been any surprises for emergency planners in Louisiana. Years earlier, the U.S. Army Corp of Engineers and the Federal Emergency Management Agency had warned that a direct strike on the City of New Orleans would cause massive flooding and possibly thousands of deaths from drowning. In fact, in a 2001 report, FEMA identified that a hurricane strike in New Orleans could be one of the three most likely devastating events to face America. The other two would be an earthquake in Los Angeles and a terrorist attack in New York. National Geographic, as well as other videographers, have produced documentaries that demonstrate the many challenges such a storm would bring to the City of New Orleans. With frightening graphics showing water rushing into downtown New Orleans, they aired their warnings at the start of every hurricane season.

There had been even more warnings just over a year earlier. "Hurricane Pam" struck the New Orleans region. She flooded the city and killed tens of thousands of unevacuated people. Luckily, she was nothing more than a fictitious storm; a statewide computer-generated Hurricane Response Drill hosted by federal, state and local emergency planners to help plan for disasters. "Hurricane Pam" demonstrated just how inadequate the region's disaster plan was for the state and many local parishes. In the absence of a realistic plan on the part of the federal, state or local leadership, it could be argued that the events that contributed to the Hurricane Katrina disaster were in place months before the 2005 hurricane season started.

Ignoring the vulnerability of a city that lies below sea level, Louisiana's Hurricane Plan put the responsibility of evacuations on the shoulders of local government and individual citizens. Many jurisdictions did take notice and developed comprehensive plans to prepare and respond to such threats. In St. Charles Parish, nearly every meeting involved computer-generated scenarios and planned for the worst. Others were complacent and did not. For New Orleans, that deadly mandate by the state spelled disaster.

The true culprit can be summed up in one word: complacency! Advanced planning was inadequate, mobilization of resources prior to the devastation was inadequate, and the ability to deal with the challenges had more to do with politics than actual need. Leadership failed to develop a clear chain of command, failed to develop a rumor control system, and failed to portray a sense of calmness and control. Instead, their actions, and failure to take action, did more to feed the pandemonium than to end it.

Months after Hurricane Katrina struck, some communities were thriving. Their rebound from a "disaster region" to a "boomtown" is directly related to pre-planning prior to the storm. Yet other areas still faced many challenges, many of which they seemed powerless to fix.

Months after the storm, Louisiana, as a whole, was fairly stable. While many New Orleanians had relocated out of state, the vast majority of the state's population remained in communities all across Louisiana. Nearly every city and town had swelled in size. Overnight, Baton Rouge had become the largest city in Louisiana. There is no doubt that New Orleans will rebuild. The question is will evacuees return to their former city? In reality, the transformation from rubble to rebound will likely create a new "New Orleans," which will bear the scars of Hurricane Katrina for decades to come.

The people of Louisiana are resilient, and simply will not accept defeat. They want to rebuild, if nothing more than to prove that they can. But in many areas, the magnitude of this event makes it virtually impossible to do so without state and federal assistance. This is especially true for those in New Orleans, where the number of residents at poverty level is far higher than the national average. In St. Bernard Parish, where every home and business flooded, there are real concerns about the ability to protect the fragile community from future storms. In Lower Plaquemines Parish, the cost of levee protection is being weighed against the number of people it would protect in the sparsely populated communities in the southern parts of that parish. Countless challenges delayed progress as these complex questions were answered.

While FEMA has done a good job in many areas of the Hurricane Katrina recovery, they have stumbled in others. There were tens of thousands of unoccupied FEMA trailers parked on vacant fields in Laurel, Mississippi, and Hope, Arkansas, waiting to be delivered to the homeless Hurricane Katrina survivors who needed a place to live. Clearly that is an unacceptable breakdown. Seven months after the storm, WWL TV, a local television news station in New Orleans, summed up the frustration in its March 29, 2006, editorial opinion:

> "When a 74-year-old Korean War vet is forced to sleep in his car because he cannot get keys to the trailer that's been in his driveway for two months, it is not enough. When a 31-year veteran of the Orleans Public School System is forced to live in her gutted home with no power or water as she waits for her trailer, it is not enough. When a family of five is forced to live in a shed as they wait for a trailer, it is not enough. For those still waiting for a trailer, the state of emergency remains in effect. It is time for it to be lifted."

Chest Deep and Rising:

Meanwhile, as FEMA struggles to fix the many problems that plague a faulty housing plan, thousands of Katrina victims are still living with family and friends.

The challenges are not limited to FEMA trailers; the process is a vicious cycle of uncertainties that made rebuilding a lesson in tenacity and more like a game of chance. For seven months after the storm, the Corp of Engineers struggled to determine the heights of Hurricane Protection Levees. FEMA needed this information to certify the flood map, and with it, the availability of Flood Insurance. The City needed all this information to set the proper building requirements. After they determined enough people would be returning to a given community to justify the resources needed to maintain City services there, then, and only then, would they issue a construction permit. Finance companies needed all this information to ensure the homes they finance will be eligible for flood insurance.

For those who wanted to return home to the worst-impacted communities, it is almost as if they can find only a couple of reasons to return and rebuild. They can, however, think of dozens of valid reasons that suggest they should focus their energies on rebuilding their lives in a more stable environment outside the city, or even the state. Many gave up in disgust and rebuilt their former homes on their own, without gaining the proper permits, and thus may not be eligible for flood insurance in the future. Other simply rebuilt their lives elsewhere. The same goes for business and industry, which had the added concern of finding a viable customer base and workforce.

Another questionable step by FEMA was most likely caused by inexperience. FEMA was stretched to the limits and needed to hire representatives by the hundreds to fill the ever-growing needs created by Hurricane Katrina and Hurricane Rita. This lack of experience and a cumbersome approval process caused much confusion. A prime example would be FEMA's refusal to permit Wal-Mart and Sam's Club stores in Jefferson Parish to reopen immediately after the evacuation bands were lifted. There was a lack of retail outlets open offering much-needed supplies to vulnerable storm victims quickly running out the essential items for survival. Receiving no reasonable explanation as to why FEMA had ordered the retailer to remain closed, Jefferson Parish Sheriff Harry Lee took matters into his own hands. Sheriff Lee announced he was "commandeering" all Sam's and Wal-Mart stores in his parish and ordered them to open as soon as possible.

The media attention created was all that was needed for FEMA to recognize its error, and the stores opened shortly after Lee's comments. But it further demonstrated the many problems created by a rigid interpretation of seemingly ever-changing regulations and little authority for representatives to offer common sense remedies.

The Heroes of Katrina

Some suggest that the vast majority of the residents of southeast Louisiana evacuated, thus saving tens of thousands of lives. Many stayed and were thrust into the middle of a deadly situation when the region began to flood. While everyone was strongly encouraged to evacuate, first responders were required to stay in harm's way as they said goodbye to family members who evacuated.

A positive "overcome and adapt" attitude adopted by first responders truly made the difference. Many first responders lost their homes, and most had significant damage. Some reports suggest that as many as 2,000 law enforcement officers were left homeless. In addition, scores of other first responders were left homeless. Yet, despite their personal crises and uncertain future, they remained on the job, rescuing, providing emergency services, and reestablishing a sense of order in a ravaged region. First responders worked around the clock and were there during the first week of the storm. They rescued the ones in need, fought lawlessness, and supplied affected areas. Anxiety was high, due to the lack of accurate information. Reports of widespread looting and attacks on first responders only raised the level of concern.

Without electricity, fuel, food and communications, they continued to patrol neighborhoods and participate in rescue missions, all the while witnessing the largest peacetime exodus of people from the New Orleans area that had ever occurred. Many volunteered for dangerous missions. Days were long and sleep was scarce. They persevered.

Local first responders rose to the challenges without the inherent governmental inertia that plagues other entities. First responders regularly respond decisively, because it is what they do every day. During the Hurricane Katrina crisis, they did it with little or no resources or communications. As Sixth District Captain Anthony Cannatella put it, first responders "held the heartbeat of the city in the palm of their hands and kept it alive."

With the exception of state and federal law enforcement agencies that played a major role in the Hurricane Katrina recovery, it was not state and federal assistance that provided the tools needed in the early days of the catastrophe. The government was overburdened with many demands as it struggled to get a handle on the enormity of the event. It was local law enforcement reaching out to their counterparts that provided the resources needed to stabilize the region. The Louisiana Sheriff's Association, National Sheriff's Association, Fraternal Order of Police, and law enforcement officers from all across the country responded en masse and provided the necessary resources to hold their ground until state and federal officers and National Guardsmen could deploy.

With tremendous displays of courage, determination, bravery and integrity, it was the police, sheriff's deputies, troopers, wildlife agents, firemen, paramedics, nurses, hospital staff, pump operators, public works staff, and public servants of all kinds who stayed to maintain their communities while everyone else was evacuated. They are the true heroes of Hurricanes Katrina and Rita. Each one of their lives is forever changed. Many will live with the scars and injuries they received; others will deal with the mental toll of the 16-day nightmare they lived through. Yet all will look at their role in the Katrina ordeal with great pride.

They stayed; they reacted; they rescued; they truly made the difference.

About the Author

Patrick Yoes is a lifelong resident of St. Charles Parish, located 20 miles west of the City of New Orleans, Louisiana. Employed by the St. Charles Sheriff's Office since 1984, Patrick has oversight of the department's Special Services Division, responsible for Community Outreach programs, and is the department's Public Information Officer. During his career with the Sheriff's Department, Patrick has worked as a patrol deputy, patrol sergeant, and detective in a department that serves as the sole law enforcement agency for St. Charles Parish's 50,000 residents.

During Hurricane Katrina, Patrick rode out the storm in a school building and responded in St. Charles Parish as the winds died down. When flooding cut off outside support to the entire region, he participated in the Fraternal Order of Police relief efforts, where he helped coordinate vital services to the officers directly in the field at the height of the chaos and during the long months of recovery that followed. He also served on the Federal Communications Commission's Independent Panel Reviewing the Impact of Hurricane Katrina on Communications Networks.

A former publisher in his family's business, the St. Charles Herald, a local newspaper that has served St. Charles Parish since 1873, Patrick has written a weekly general interest editorial column that details life in and around St. Charles

Parish and southeast Louisiana, for over 17 years.

Patrick has served on the National Executive Board of the 324,000-member Fraternal Order of Police since 2003 and presently serves as National Secretary. He also serves as President of the Louisiana State Lodge Fraternal Order of Police, a position he has held since 2001.

Patrick received an Associate Degree in Criminal Justice from Nicholls State University and is a graduate of the 196th session of the FBI National Academy in Quantico, VA. He and his family reside in Norco, Louisiana.